The Elixir *of* Truth

JOURNEY ON THE SUFI PATH

VOLUME ONE

Musa Muhaiyaddeen
(E. L. Levin)

THE WITNESS WITHIN INC.

I would like to give special thanks to my editor, Sharon Marcus, my production coordinator, Amy Wilson, my graphic designer, Lawrence Didona and to my photographer, Lou Wilson.

Audio discourses in English are available at **www.thewitnesswithin.com**

Library of Congress Control Number: 2013933544

Muhaiyaddeen, Musa

The Elixir of Truth: Journey on the Sufi Path, Volume 1/
Musa Muhaiyaddeen (E. L. Levin)
Atlantic City, NJ: The Witness Within, Inc., 2013
p. cm.

Trade paperback: 978-0-9890185-0-0
Also available in Kindle, Epub and iPad formats.

1. Sufism. 2. God. 3. Truth. 4. Wisdom. 5. Reality. 6. Enlightenment.
7. Eternal Life. 8. Transformation. I. Title

Printed in the United States of America
First Printing

This book is dedicated to my teacher,
Muhammad Raheem Bawa Muhaiyaddeen,
my wife, Asiya
and my parents.

Table of Contents

Introduction

In the name of God, Most Merciful, Most Compassionate. I was raised on a farm in a small community in Southern New Jersey. I did the usual things a young person does in America. I played baseball, I played football, I watched television, I listened to rock and roll, I went to school. After high school, I went on to university and then to graduate school.

When I was in graduate school, the youth of America were erupting into what may be called America's cultural revolution. Ideas as to what was important in life and attitudes towards life in general were beginning to change. I was intrigued by all of these ideas. I began to question the reasons for existence. People were marching for civil liberties and against war. I was in the midst of constant eruptions of thoughts and ideas that threatened the very core of what was considered stability.

It was becoming more and more apparent to me that most people did not understand the nature of existence. Even though people did not know what they were talking about it did not stop them from believing that they had answers. This is not to say that they were trying to lie to me. It just means they were giving me answers to questions according to their own level of understanding. In essence, they were doing the best they could. This was not satisfactory to me.

I began on a course to find real answers to my questions.

Questions like, why am I here? What is the purpose of my creation? What is my relationship to my Creator? What is our true relationship with the rest of mankind? How are we supposed to act? What is my destiny?

I was looking for someone who would actually tell me the truth. What does a human being who understands the answers to these questions look like? What is the essence of one who understands the answers to these questions? I was looking for the truth based in reality, not based on fictitious imaginations of the people I had been talking to. I began to read and read, and ran across a phrase that I prayed would apply to me, "When you are ready for a teacher, a teacher will appear for you."

In March of 1972 I was living near Philadelphia, Pennsylvania and got word that a teacher had somehow landed there. I went to see him. He was a small, dark-complexioned man from Sri Lanka who spoke a language called Tamil. When I first stepped into his presence I knew something was different. I could not put it into words, but I knew it. I was now in front of someone who was based in reality. I was in front of someone who was different from anyone else I had ever met. I had questions which I did not ask because I was stunned into silence by his presence. The unasked questions were answered. I knew I had met my teacher, I was thirsty for what he had to offer. A new level of energy and excitement entered into my being. I had never encountered a situation this intense, a situation that I could not get enough of.

It became incredibly important to me to be in front of him, to be near him, to be in his presence, to be surrounded by his essence. There was nowhere else that I wanted to be, there was nowhere else that I needed to go. When I was with him it was apparent to me that I was in the center of the universe, I was protected, I was looked after. I was a child again, once again being taught, but this time being taught the nature of truth and reality.

This relationship lasted fourteen years until my teacher passed from this world in December of 1986. Over the fourteen years with my teacher he taught me what a person needs to do to become a true human being. He showed me what a true human being looked like. He became the mirror so that I could see what I was supposed to become. His name was Muhammad Raheem Bawa Muhaiyaddeen. He was love personified, he was mercy personified, he was compassion personified. He said that we could become like him, he said that we should become like him. He brought me close to him and within the first few weeks after I met him, he instructed me to talk about what he had taught me to others. I began doing so almost immediately.

What he brought into this world is very special. God in His mercy continues to send those with the knowledge of God into this world to teach men about their Creator and to teach men how to become true human beings and enter reality. Man is God's penultimate creation. Man, however, has lost his way and needs to be returned to his birthright. My teacher was among those who were sent to teach us our birthright. Our birthright is to be elevated from lower animal consciousness to elevated consciousness or wisdom, so that we can know our Lord and know reality.

The talks in this book are about the transformation that needs to take place for us to become a true human being, they are about purification, they are about the path that God has given to us. It is my intention that these words are helpful to humanity. We ask the blessings of my teacher, the friends of God and the prophets in this effort.

Musa Muhaiyaddeen

The Journey

Man's destiny is directly related to his state of consciousness. As man moves from a desire filled egocentric consciousness towards the various exalted levels of wisdom he transcends his illusory worldly circumstances and moves towards his true destiny in reality. Man's real work in this world is this transformation of his consciousness from animal qualities to the light filled wisdom that is free of elemental influences and resides within the grace filled qualities of God.

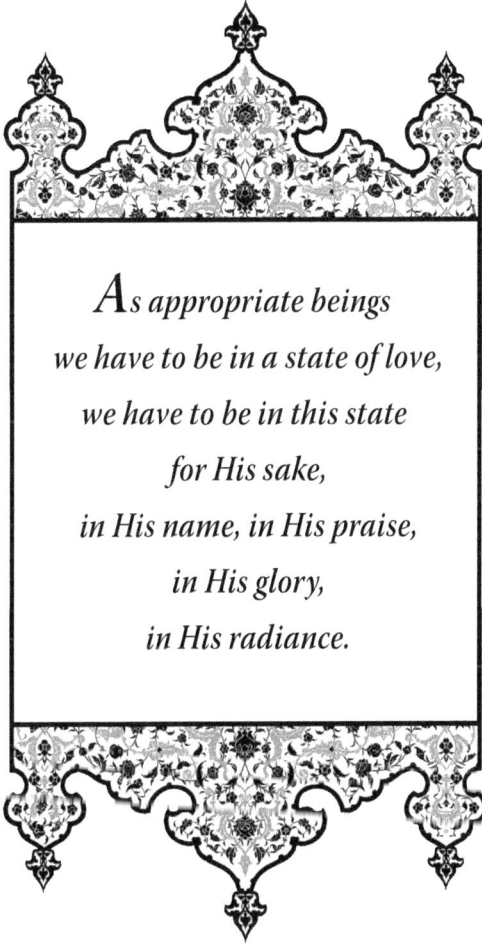

As appropriate beings
we have to be in a state of love,
we have to be in this state
for His sake,
in His name, in His praise,
in His glory,
in His radiance.

Understanding Love

When we set out on this path to reality there are certain fundamental questions we have to ask ourselves: who am I, why am I here, what is the purpose of creation, why was I created, what is the purpose of existence, what is the purpose of this life? The answers are easy, living the answers is difficult. We are here because of God's love, we were created through His love, we exist because of love, we came from love, we are love, our intention is to return to love.

This love we talk about is a powerful yet elusive quality. We have all used the word love, we have all been in love, we have all been in love with love, we all have had some experience of love in our life, but have we ever focused on love as the reason for existence, on love as the core of existence, love as the power keeping electrons within atoms in the place where they are meant to be? What is this love, how do we become part of this love, what does it do to us, do for us, through us? How are we in touch with this love, how do we understand it, what does it mean?

When we contemplate a field of flowers off in the distance on a bright sunny day, we see the horizon, the different colors of the flowers and grasses, the gentle movement of the plants and small animals, we experience a sense of peace, of serenity. If that serenity grows and becomes luminous we have a sense of integration in an aspect of serenity itself, we feel as if we are part of the force driving that serenity, producing it. This is a taste of love. When we see a baby whose joyful laughter makes us smile automatically, for no reason other than the beauty of the baby's existence, this is a taste of love. When we observe a gracious act which is totally selfless, understanding what has occurred at that moment, understanding it as something done on behalf of our Creator for the sake of His creation, done by a person who realizes the connection between the Creator and creation, we have a glimpse of love.

When we remember that God created us so that we can know Him, that He has given us the gift of understanding, of being able to understand His qualities of compassion and mercy, this is the fragrance of love. When we sit in front of a great saint who looks at us with pleasure, a spark flies across the room with a smile that makes our heart pound faster, this is a realization of love. When we leave everything restricting us behind, when we abandon our worries and release the burdens of anxiety, when we are free in the moment, we are swimming in love.

Love is what we live in, what we live for. The veils we create are like body armor keeping us away from love; we need to remove that armor. God constantly sends His vibration, His resonance of love into the world which is invigorated by His love at every nanosecond, yet humanity takes up arms to fight against this love. We do not have the patience to sit still and catch the scent of love, we do not have the patience to sit still to witness love. Instead, we take up arms to protect what we have created, believing it to be more important than love. The things we consider more important than love differ around the world in accordance with the culture we are born to, the place we live and the quality of life in that place.

In the midst of this holy love steadily sent here, man habitually commits vile acts. Our ability to ignore reality and live in our own constructs is overwhelming, it brings tears to those who live in this holy love; our capacity to make hell out of heaven is so abundant it buckles the knees of those who are holy. Some who are hidden sit in prayer asking the rest of humanity to see what they see, asking the rest of humanity to understand what they understand, to feel the vibratory resonance they feel.

Perfection exists around us yet we insist on imperfection. If inner patience and absolute contentment were in the hearts of human beings, it would change the world so radically we would no longer have the problems all around us now, if we had the patience to sit still for a week everything would change, but we do not sit still for a minute. The mind which never stops creates the illusions of reality we respond to. When people ask how to stop listening to the mind, the answer is given in their question, stop listening to it. We know the mind is there, we know it is making us mad and foolish by telling us to do things we should not do, certain things we do not care about yet still do.

The ultimate answer sounds too simple, nevertheless, the root of the answer is that we do not know how to love on a greater scale, we do not know how to love for the sake of God. We love for ourselves, our love is selfish love for the sake of the things we think we need, the things we have made important in our life, the things we believe sustain us, that carry us from day to day.

People who have given some thought to their lives, people who have focused on this, understand that the only moments they have truly lived are those transcendent moments when they are aligned with truth, when they exist in reality. We spend a lifetime worrying, thinking about and paying homage to all those things that do not matter because we do not know how to stop. Stop just means stop, there are no options for certain things we need to stop, need to change. As long as we believe we have options, as long as we choose not to do the appropriate things we need to do, then what is truly appropriate for our life will not have the space to happen.

To be doing what is appropriate means becoming appropriate beings. As appropriate beings we have to be in a state of love, we have to be in this state for His sake, in His name, in His praise, in His glory, in His radiance. When we understand this and make it our reason for existence we become appropriate, as we become appropriate our acts become appropriate, our essence becomes appropriate and we exist in reality. Until this happens we do not exist in reality.

There are some societies or groups which will not admit

us unless we have reached certain levels of realization, some groups have first, second and third degree memberships. We are told the world has seventy-three groups or tribes, only one of which is acceptable to God. The one acceptable to God is the one which is appropriate for God, and we need to reach that state of appropriateness. How do we do that? We do that by accepting Him, by allowing Him in our life in such a way that when we give something to Him, we give Him back to Himself, then we are appropriate.

We become appropriate when God walks with us, God's resonance moves within us. We need to recognize this in ourselves and in our friends and companions, encouraging this in ourselves and in them, praising what is worthy of praise and staying away from what is not. We should realize what is worthy and take appropriate action at the right time so that everything appropriate exists within us.

This is the work of this path, the work of those who choose the path to reality. There are many things we can look for in this world; if we are searching for reality the key to it means existing in it. The great mystery on this path is that we have to become the key, it is not handed to us, it is not given to us nor is it found. We are the key—when we change we unlock the door, everything appears the same from the outside, but everything is now different. The difference is that we exist in reality. We do not see others as different from ourselves, hunger is not something someone else has and I do not, pain is not something someone else has and I do not. In reality there is unity, if we are in reality there is unity in our state of being, unity between ourselves and those God has put us together with.

The places where we have been put, the people we have met, the people we have been given, the relationships we are involved with, they are the ones we are supposed to have, but we are supposed to deal with all of them appropriately, we are supposed to deal with them in reality. As that reality grows, as we are closer to it, we perceive the difference, the air is different, what we see is different, whom we see and how we see them are different because in reality we are engulfed in love, we see through eyes which love as God loves, as a holy being loves, we love like lovers of God. Things slow down, there is no rush, there is nowhere else to be because we are already there. The world exists and we are part of it in the truest sense.

May the love which makes us keys to reality enter our state, transform us at the cellular level so that it touches our true spirit, every atom in our existence. May we exult in this love, understand its warmth, its nurturing, understand its inherent goodness, and may that goodness become who we are.

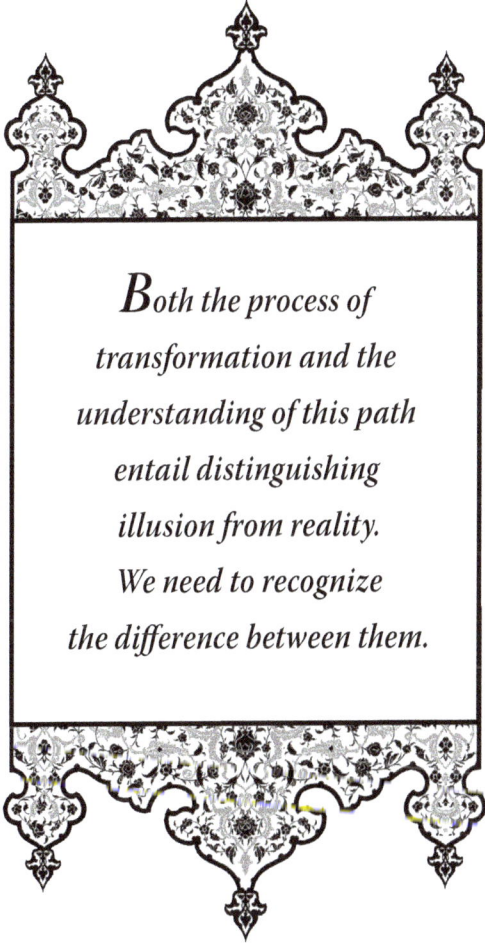

Both the process of transformation and the understanding of this path entail distinguishing illusion from reality. We need to recognize the difference between them.

CHAPTER TWO

Unlocking Reality

We have a set of beliefs which has shaped our life, beliefs which might be deeply established or ready for modification. But just because we have maintained this structure, this set of beliefs, that does not confer validity. To change what we believe in, to alter or give up what we believe and understand in a new way is difficult, our beliefs were established when we were very young. What we learn when we are young is deeply ingrained in us. We are imprinted profoundly when we are young. It is time to ask if we were imprinted appropriately or inappropriately. If it was inappropriate we might have accepted beliefs which run counter to our own well-being or to an understanding of reality.

When we believe something to be true we will not see anything negative in it—this is our blind spot, what we believe in. We cling to that blind spot imprinted on us when we were young. Both the process of transformation and the understanding of this path entail distinguishing illusion from reality, we need to recognize the difference between them. Some know what they should not do but fail to act on that knowledge, they rationalize their actions to make them conform with whatever they have taken as emotional satisfaction. They refuse to alter something imprinted in childhood.

One key to unlocking the door to reality is wanting to, it can actually be that easy, but this is not as easy as it sounds because truly wanting God, wanting His reality, wanting to give up the illusions we have been raised with, the hypnotic fascinations of the world, that magnetic pull of everything attracting us, all that is difficult to do. The words are easy enough to say: a key to entering reality is truly wanting to, the difficulty lies in understanding what this entails and then acting on our understanding. To leave the duality of our existence behind, to bypass all the clamoring inner voices saying I need, I want, I desire, I must have, I cannot do without, to leave those voices behind and focus instead on the reason for existence, this is the way to know God. Focusing on that, making that our reality is what we have to do, this is what lies at the heart of transformation.

This is a different path for each of us, even though it is remarkably the same. To a certain extent we all see the same things, although we see colors a little differently, we measure distances a little differently. Some see more clearly, some less, yet we see what we are looking at in a similar way. We might need a little correction, we might need a few things pointed out to us, but if we had to say what a table looks like we would agree. If it came to how we see the table in our own context, in relation to ourselves or inside our own head, the answers might have nothing to do with the table itself, with what is going outwardly, the answers might depend on the breadth, the length and width of our experience, our interactions with others and how we handle or assimilate them. Our answers could depend on what we consider important, our priorities, our qualities. There would be a different story from each of us, some not even comprehensible. It can take a long time to explain how we actually see and understand.

If this is so difficult to explain to someone else, do we really think we understand ourselves, do we think we recognize what goes on inside us, do we make sensible conclusions about what is going on, or do we deduce what goes on according to our established priorities? Have the early controlling influences which have brought us this far been so deeply entrenched we have trouble turning away from them? When we make a decision do we contemplate a list of priorities or is everything on automatic, without reference to its effect on the next moment? Every action is a precursor to the next, every thought is a precursor to the next, every emotion, every situation, every attitude is a precursor to the next. We ignite our own fires or we put them out. If we accumulate a certain amount of anger we are setting fire to something, will it be ourselves, our spouse, someone we see on the street, the next person we meet no matter who they are? We have accumulated anger which has to be released somewhere or has to be eliminated. The relations we have with other people might have nothing to do with them, it might be more relevant to whatever we have allowed to brew inside us.

We are our own chemistry lab where we make the mixtures resulting in ourselves, who we are, who we will be. We create ourselves with our actions, every moment is an opportunity to re-create ourselves, every moment is an opportunity to create the true intention to know reality. Every moment is an opportunity to contemplate mercy, forgiveness, compassion, generosity. Think about the opportunity renewing itself with every breath, an opportunity to enter reality. What is the key? The key is the intention to go there, establishing a fervent desire to go there. We have learned something about desire, about lust and greed. We know the places desire can take us, we know what it feels like. Transform these desires into wanting God. We have recognized desire, reacted to it, and yet we have not experienced it appropriately, we have not put it to work in the right way, even though we have the tools. We have tools we have played with all our lives, now we must use them appropriately. This means giving up that original set of beliefs, finding a new way.

There is something beyond the door we are about to pass through we have not experienced yet, something we do not know, something we cannot imagine or be intuitive about without falling back into illusion, creating the moment instead of allowing God to create it for us. If we think we know we have entered illusion, if we think we understand what will happen next we are creating illusion, creating reality instead of allowing it. If we stop thinking we know, this is surrender. If we say God, we do not know, show us, we have no preconception, show us, then we empty our cup. There is no room in a cup already full. If we know what is going to happen next we have blocked the doorway, nothing can be added, we do not truly want to know because we know already. All this goes on internally, it cannot be faked, it is self-regulating, either we empty the cup or we do not. If it is already full nothing new can come in. Once we see this we understand that we ourselves are standing in our way, that we have to get out of the way.

What do we do with all these systems of belief stopping us? Either we dig and dig slowly until we find our way out, or else we can actually pull out whole systems by the root and discard them. We might think we are also throwing away certain things we thought were right, but there will not be much. A wise teacher advises us to pull them out, throw them away. To be rid of all that we need to discard we have to understand the overwhelming nature of our arrogance, our self-deception. For many of us arrogance is our backbone, if we let it go we crumble, this is what holds us up. Understand that we do not need this, there is something much greater than arrogance holding us together, something much greater than our belief in the self holding us together. As long as we do not accept this, arrogance remains our backbone, it does hold us up, it creates who we are without a way to escape. When this changes we change, our backbone is no longer arrogance, our backbone is absolute faith, the faith, certitude and determination that God is One. He is real, He exists within us and sustains us. Our actions are through Him, by Him, because of Him.

This is transformation, alteration, this is true change, the salvation each moment offers. We have been given this moment to unlock our understanding of reality. If it does not happen at this moment we have been given the next, breath after breath, to introduce a new belief, to sustain our path to reality. May this be easy for us.

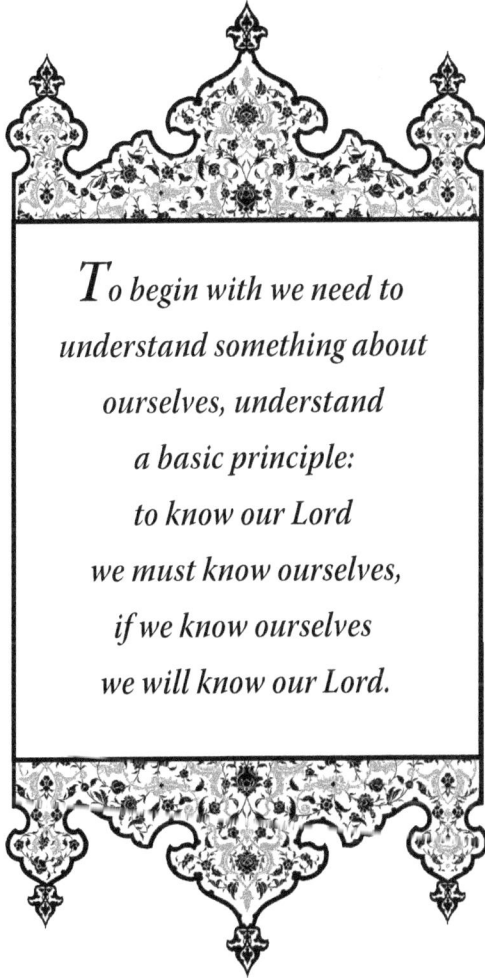

*To begin with we need to
understand something about
ourselves, understand
a basic principle:
to know our Lord
we must know ourselves,
if we know ourselves
we will know our Lord.*

Path of Transformation

This is a path of transformation, a path of doing, not talking, a path of genuine work, things we have to do. What we do is not so much something to talk about, it is something to become. Using the word transformation means we have to understand where are we going, where it takes us, what needs to be transformed, and most important, how it occurs, how and why we undertake this transformation. What purpose does the process serve, why should we undertake it?

To begin with we need to understand something about ourselves, understand a basic principle: to know our Lord we must know ourselves, if we know ourselves we will know our Lord. We ourselves initiate this work, it is not forced on us. It might seem strange to some people that we do not know ourselves, they might think this does not make sense, it is not a necessary investigation, but the popularity of psychoanalysis should remind us there is a need to understand what motivates us. Once we undertake this understanding of ourselves we recognize we do not always know why we do the things we do, there is often no simple explanation for us or for anyone else. Understanding others is another question, however, to begin with we have to approach understanding ourselves.

Scriptures, prophets and great, holy beings have given us information to help us understand who we are. Essentially, they tell us we have two aspects, the undifferentiated soul connected to God, that aspect of God given to us at birth, and the differentiated self, the animal portion of our being. We need to learn something about this animal portion of ourselves because the animal and nonanimal act in different ways. The undifferentiated soul and the differentiated aspect of ourselves have different intentions, different actions, and different reasons for existence.

When we know ourselves we discover that the true part of who we are is the eternal part, the undifferentiated, the soul. The other part is not our true self, yet during the course of our life we come to believe this individuated aspect, this egocentric self, these animal qualities are who we are. Why do we make this identification with the animal aspect, with the individuated, egocentric self, and not with the undifferentiated, God-self portion? This has something to do with the way we are brought up, the things we are taught when we are young. If we are not taught to be God-centered, if we are not taught our true nature we limit our existence in the world with an agenda, things we need to accomplish, to fulfill. We need to feed ourselves, clothe ourselves, find shelter, support ourselves and our family.

These basic instincts are no different from an animal's requirements. A bear procreates, finds shelter and food. We have all seen pictures of bears sitting beside a river pulling out the salmon. This process engages their intellect—they have to figure out how to catch things, how to fish and how to know where the fish are found. They do not simply stand there with their mouths open waiting to be fed. We are like the animals in this, figuring out that we need something and learning how to get it. Learning how to fulfill a need, how to satisfy a drive is the activity of what we call intellect. We are so proud of this intellect because we are so much more advanced than animals, yet it is their intellect that serves them well to satisfy their needs.

This drive to fulfill our desires, to satisfy certain instinctual needs is basic, a level which entails fulfilling one's own needs, not someone else's which are unimportant to us compared with our own. If we watch a bear fishing we do not see it catch the salmon and give it away, this does not happen when survival of the self is so instinctively important. To be integrated with others, to feel the difficulties of others, to be in that undifferentiated place where our skin does not separate us is not common among people. We should try to understand why this is.

When we were created the whole universe was placed in our heart. We have everything in existence within us, all the animals, animal tendencies and animal qualities. This egocentric animal has no interest in learning something about its connection to God, it does not have the morality of a God-centered understanding. If a snake feels threatened it will kill anything in its way. Each animal has specific qualities, a deer protects itself by running away, a bull protects itself by charging. Animals have different inclinations but the result is the same, protection of the self without concern for what it encounters. Do you think a bull cares for what it butts, do you think a lion cares for the life it eats, do you think a hyena worries about stealing its food from a lion? Hunger is paramount, they have no such concern.

Raised without an understanding of the undifferentiated self, we find it difficult to understand there is more to us than our animal nature, our animal self. Still, to understand that there is more, we do have to understand that animal self. Now many animals do not seem dangerous, rabbits do not seem dangerous except if they invade our vegetable garden threatening our food supply, deer do not seem dangerous unless they destroy our crops

Understand that the undifferentiated soul is the crop of our true sustenance, it is the point where eternity is available through our connection to God, and unless we make that connection, with all these animals running around inside us, our consciousness is their consciousness. When we are only interested in food, the need for food and how to get it is who we are, when we are only interested in sex, if that is our focus we are out of control. Compare the sexual excitement of rutting animals, they are wild and out of control. When our instinctual nature pushes so hard we have no other thought, we are like the animals.

We are all a little different from each other, perhaps we are like different animals, a deer, a bull, or we might be arrogant like an elephant or a crocodile. Will a crocodile or a hippopotamus back off? Nothing stops them. Then there are those who are timid, they might run away but they do what they do in hidden corners, not out in the open, another way of fulfilling individual needs. That animal consciousness is strengthened when we allow it, when we give it space to become the focus of our consciousness. If we try to dislodge the animal it bites, like any other animal it does not want to die, it wants to dominate our consciousness, keep us in its control. The path of transformation means understanding ourselves, it means finding, engaging and struggling with our controlling animals.

We can imagine what it is like to fight a huge Kodiak bear, but what about a rabbit, it doesn't seem hard to deal with a rabbit, it doesn't seem we need protection from a rabbit, yet we still have to fence it out, keep it from that constant nibbling. Someone who does not eat large meals but nibbles all day can gain just as much weight as the person who eats heavy meals. If this is our problem we have to fence off the rabbit. We must encounter these inner animals which bare their teeth in a ferocious struggle like any wild animal. It does not matter how small they are, think of a rat or a badger. They are frightened, they do not want to back off, they want to live, they do not want you to kill them.

We need a certain courage to face these inner animals, either we let them dominate our consciousness or there is a fight. Trying to take a salmon from the Kodiak is like trying to wrest our consciousness from the inner bear, from the inner lion or hyena. This confrontation is what our transformation is about. If we do not believe we have these tendencies we have lost the battle, if we do not go searching for these tendencies we have already lost the battle.

We have seen that animals can be tamed, we have seen the wildest animals tamed. We have to be kind, we have to love the tamed animals because those beaten into submission readily revert to their wild state. This means we should learn how to confront our inner animals correctly, how to recognize them, look them in the face and offer love even though they are sworn enemies. Since they want to live they do not want us to exist. That part of us which is truly who we are, the part we are searching for and want to become has nothing to do with animals, it lies far beyond them.

This part of us is something which gives instead of taking, it loves instead of fighting, it uses wisdom instead of intellect. This part of us is something which does not try to calculate what I need for me because it understands the undifferentiated nature of us all. If we want to enter that undifferentiated state, that state which is His glory, His radiance and His truth, we must move away from any state attached to the world. Our animal qualities attach us to the world, unless we make the effort to find and confront them we remain in their control.

When we live in a jungle and we need to eat, we need to sustain ourselves, we should know the creatures who live there if we do not want to become their food. We have to know the dangers confronting us, know where we can go, where we cannot go, what we can and cannot do or we are in serious trouble. We all live in a jungle, the jungle of the mind where every animal exists. If we are to escape and move into the clear, open space we must know how to handle the animals, how to deal with them. When they occupy our consciousness we think they are who we are, and we are lost, we become lions, we become deceivers or false prophets. Since that is who we are we can only offer animal motivation, we can only give what we have. A poisonous snake can only offer venom, if we have acquired the qualities of a poisonous snake all we can bring to a situation is venom, if we have acquired the qualities of a hyena all we can bring is deception. We are dishonest because animals do not have any concept of honesty, it has no meaning for them, it is irrelevant. A fox has no morality, morality does not exist for animals. They need to eat, everything else is secondary. We need to eat too, but in a way which includes regard for others, we need to provide for ourselves, but in an honest, moral way. This path leading from the jungle starts with an understanding that the rules are different for man and animals. Once we accept animal rules for ourselves we begin the descent to an animal form.

We should learn the discipline of behavior and attitude, the first steps on our path. Conscience does not develop immediately, this conscience which tells us what is right and what is wrong arrives at the level of consciousness which understands there is more to life than desire and its fulfillment. Once we know this we can learn the difference between right and wrong, we can integrate that wisdom in our consciousness and actually become what is right. This consciousness cannot be something we are just told about, it has to be as instinctive as animal qualities are for animals. Conscience means we do automatically what is correct, we are connected to what is correct because here we find our true treasure, here in that eternal, undifferentiated soul.

An animal's existence is tied to its immediate needs. When we go beyond those levels of consciousness which only understand desire we recognize there is more, but we do have to go beyond those levels. We must enter the state in which the undifferentiated soul understands the grace and glory of love, understands what it can do, the place where it can take us, that place we need to be transformed to enter, that place of love. In the place where love becomes the reason for our existence, and that love is the reason that creation exists, the reason why God created us, in this place God lets us taste His essence, He lets us taste His compassion, His holy names of grace. We can know those holy names, He lets us taste His compassion, His patience, His gentleness, tolerance and justice. We can be these qualities and taste their glory. We can develop a thirst for this by realizing what the other qualities are and where they take us.

We can use some aspect of the qualities we used as animals on our path to God, we can make our desire a desire for God. Some of the tools we are shown in the world can be used in a permissible way to search for God. May those permissible tools be our hands, our eyes, our mouth and ears, used correctly in His service and His glory.

*If we are controlled by our
comfort zone, the familiar,
if we are drawn to things we
already understand or
think we understand,
our eyes are closed to other
possibilities.
We need to recognize that
we have the tendency to close our
own eyes, we have that tendency
because we want to be calm,
we do not want anything which
makes us uncomfortable,
anything which causes change.*

Keeping Our Eyes Open

Jesus said seek and ye shall find. To look for something our eyes have to be open, if they are not we are unable to see, whatever we are looking for is just not visible. Just as we have to look on the outside, we also have to look within, we have to see what lies within, inside.

What does all this seeing mean? We have been told we must see with an inner eye, the eye within the eye, we must hear with an inner ear, the ear within the ear. We have to be aware of this, our wisdom must know how to look beyond the surface of things. First we see the surface, the outer, then if we take the time to study, to look deeper, we understand more of the truth. This process initially includes an assumption that we can learn more, that what there is to know is not all revealed at once. When the prophet Muhammad was asked why it took him so long to assume his prophethood, he said an oak tree does not become an oak overnight. Elsewhere, he also said when we are asked to make a decision it is a good idea to wait for three days, this gives us the opportunity to reflect on our decisions, to look deeply into a situation before offering a response.

These examples mean we have to look appropriately to find something. Next, consider what we are looking for, if we are not looking for the right thing no matter how much we seek we will never find anything important. What are we really looking for, how correctly attuned are we to the object of our search, how open are we? The truth comes in different packages, in the way God presents it to us, but if we expect it to arrive in a certain way we could well be the very thing blocking it. In 1972 when I met Bawa Muhaiyaddeen, a small man from a little island I knew as Ceylon from my stamp collecting days, it was evident that here was someone extraordinary, someone from outside my own culture, outside any religion I had known. He did not speak a language I knew, he did not look like anyone I knew, he was different from any person I had ever spoken to. The situation was completely unfamiliar, coming from a place I did not expect, yet I understood immediately here was something important. I had a choice to make, did I want to stay in my comfort zone or did I want to go somewhere I knew nothing about, put energy into learning something absolutely new, in an entirely different situation where I knew nothing, or would I leave and go back to what I knew?

This is relevant to keeping our eyes open. If we are controlled by our comfort zone, the familiar, if we are drawn to things we already understand or think we understand, our eyes are closed to other possibilities. We need to recognize that we have a tendency to close our own eyes, we have that tendency because we want to be calm, we do not want anything which makes us uncomfortable, anything which causes change. Change means giving up things we like, things we find comfortable, the things we know, it means giving them up to enter an open space we are unfamiliar with, a space evoking memories of discomfort. This discomfort is like the first day in a new school, or at college where there is no one we know. When we live in a way which keeps us on the edge, where we keep going beyond our comfort zone to places we have not been before, when we go voluntarily because we understand this discomfort is one way progress can occur, we learn something important about walking on the edge. We must watch where we go so that we do not fall in, keep our eyes wide open to see where we are going. Keeping our eyes open, we cannot be afraid of what we might see. If fear overwhelms us, if we see something we find uncomfortable and close our eyes, we turn around, we walk away.

There are things we should shut our eyes against, things which are unacceptable, not things which are uncomfortable, there is a difference. Know the difference between what is unacceptable and what is the edge of our comfort zone, especially since today's comfort zone is defined as the essence of success. Not having to do anything, lying on a beach without thought, surrendering to the pleasure of the sun and the water, being catered to, all that is defined as comfort. This means turning away from everything actually going on, no real integration with existence, a failure to be fully alive, to understand the cycle of life. When our eyes are open we see this comfort is nothing but a lie, the advertising. Advertising depends on keeping our eyes closed, it makes money if we cannot see. Once we see, we recognize the manipulation.

When we think about the word sin we think of it as some great violation of God's law, acting against The Commandments which list them. We forget the first two and remember only those which tell us not to bear false witness, not to covet our neighbor's wife, not to murder. The first one, the one that says there is one God and we should have no other God, this is the one we usually forget. There is another way to say we should have no other God, and that is we should not be distracted. Anything that is not God, anything we place ahead of God is a distraction. We think we conform to God's commandments because we do not steal, we do not commit adultery, we do not covet our neighbor's wife, but we are distracted. In that distraction we have violated the first commandment. If we were not distracted it would never occur to us to do any of the unacceptable things rising from our distractions. Forbidden things present themselves because we succumb to the power of the world.

What keeps our eyes open? We can start by keeping our eyes open to ourselves, observing how we act, seeing what influences us, what is good for us, what is bad for us. Then we can keep our eyes open to the good, closed to the bad, and then we can learn to do this consistently, without distraction. If we are distracted as we walk along the edge, we fall in. Many scientists today have no belief in God, scientists who insist their theories alone are true, provable. Yet we have had scientists like Albert Einstein and Max Planck who walked the edge, who formulated the very theories other scientists still study. Those who walked the edge realized they knew very little, they were conjecturing the best way they could within the limits of their understanding. Lesser scientists who follow up these theories experimentally are different from those on the edge, they cannot find the edge itself because their eyes are not open enough to see it.

Since they do not see the edge, they think there is no such thing. They think they know, they think differently from someone at the edge—a person at the edge can see that he does not know, his eyes are wide open, he is a believer like Einstein and Planck. Many who came after them have been lost in arrogance, their eyes are not open enough to see beyond their outer vision which does not include everything, something they fail to understand. When our vision is limited we make assumptions based on that limited vision. We must extend our vision beyond the physical; once we limit ourselves to physical vision alone without opening our eyes to the inner, we place limitations upon ourselves. We have decisions to make, we must decide what we will do with our life, who we will become, how we will live.

We have to open our eyes to what our society calls normal behavior, behavior defined in terms of its own idiosyncrasies, its own incorrect behavior which it labels normal. If we live in this society with our eyes open to the truth, we have to understand something might be politically correct but not necessarily either correct or true. We cannot merely accept what everyone else does, everything must be examined. There are so many choices to make about reality. In this country we allow these choices, and we need them all for the truth to have a place to live. In a place where choice is not permitted there is a good chance that truth will be stifled, we might be killed for walking through the doors of truth.

The gratification of pleasure is not the purpose of our existence, our purpose is to know who we really are, and we are not this being of flesh, we are a being of light. Until we understand this light being we do not know the truth about ourselves, we have limited ourselves to the knowledge of the senses. We exist beyond our senses; the universe, all that exists and all that can be exists within us. Once we understand this, we have an appropriate view of who we are, we can keep our eyes open.

We should look at what addresses us, talks to us, and notice where it comes from, see how it has become part of our life, our state of being. Examine it, see what it does to us, how it makes us react. If something does not make us react appropriately throw it out, reject it. When we recognize that something affects us inappropriately get rid of it, always remembering how hard it is to be rid of these things. Realize it is a struggle, it is not easy, but we have been given the tools, the weapons for this struggle, our own inner war. May God give us the courage to fight and win this battle.

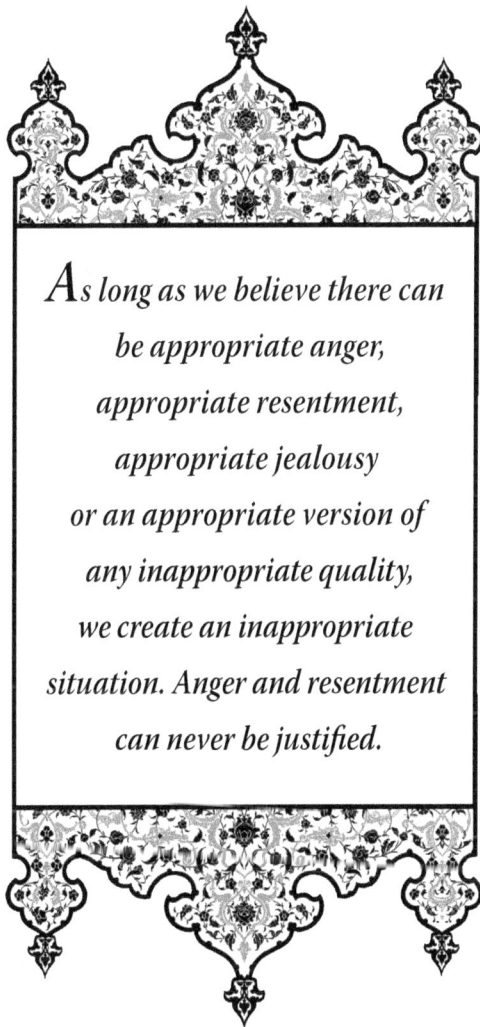

*As long as we believe there can
be appropriate anger,
appropriate resentment,
appropriate jealousy
or an appropriate version of
any inappropriate quality,
we create an inappropriate
situation. Anger and resentment
can never be justified.*

Elemental Conflicts

A wise man was once asked, "When will we have peace?" He answered, "A man will be at peace when he sits in the sun and has no desire to sit in the shade, when he sits in the shade he will have no desire to sit in the sun."

People think peace is found by adjusting the circumstances to suit their definition of peace. What happens inwardly during this adjusting of circumstances makes it impossible to be peaceful: when we are uncomfortable in a situation certain emotional, elemental disturbances erupt inside us which make us react, then we think it is up to us to alter the circumstances, to adjust things so that we can be at peace.

Here is the confusion, sometimes there are external circumstances which need to be altered, sometimes not. We need to know when we should insist and when we should not, most of the time we do not need to interfere. We need to learn how to see perfection, the inability to see perfection is our difficulty, not the circumstances we are dealing with. Although we think the problem lies in our circumstances, we are what needs changing, we have to develop the ability to deal with circumstances without inner eruptions. This is a different way of looking at things, an important understanding of self-discovery, the understanding that everything exists within. If we think that things exist on the outside we keep trying to adjust what is outside, yet what lies outside usually cannot be adjusted, it remains in turmoil.

Try changing the weather, try making it what we prefer. We know it's warmer in Florida than in Alaska, if we want to be warm there's a better chance of being warm in Florida than Alaska. If we want to be warm in Alaska we will have a hard time, an inner disruption. There are difficulties in Florida too, hurricanes and tumultuous storms can happen in warm or cold weather, there are such things as weather difficulties. We recognize natural occurrences in the elements, those outer forms which are in a state of constant flux or conflict, tornadoes, hurricanes, floods, rains, volcanoes, all these things happen. The same elemental things happen inside us—on the outside we call the eruption of a mountain a volcano, on the inside we call the eruption anger; what we call a hurricane on the outside may be called hatred on the inside. We have inner elemental eruptions which we often blame on something happening outside.

Elemental eruptions can manifest as physical conflicts among people or as conflicts among ideas. Most ideological conflicts have more to do with conflicts among people rather than ideas, more to do with satisfying a sense of peace in conflicting individuals. Where there is love we see a much greater capacity to endure difficulty. Babies cause endless difficulty, they scream, they cry, they have to be cleaned, they need nonstop attention. What do we think about an adult who needs this kind of attention? If it is someone we love we might handle it for awhile, if it is someone we do not love, when the attention demanded is greater than we are prepared to offer, it is hard to be involved, hard to be at peace. This comes back to finding peace within ourselves instead of looking for it outside, this is a key to peace. The more we focus on inner repose the more we understand where peace exists.

In prayer we alter the nature of our interaction with the world, we withdraw from the conflicts of life by focusing on a higher Being, surrendering to that higher Being, to His trust and care. The ability to release ourselves from interacting with external things, leaving all that in God's hands, changes our elemental nature. By surrendering we are connected to the underlying perfection of everything, matching our vibration to that vibration, and we can find peace, we are at rest. Things like anxiety, anger, resentment just leave.

Some people go through their lives in turmoil believing turmoil is justifiable, believing they have earned it in a noble way— it is appropriate because they are righteously creating a righteous situation. But we are what we carry around, we are our qualities; if we walk around with resentment, whether we think it is righteous or not, it is still resentment. When someone has wronged us deeply and we resent the wrong, if we hold onto resentment it is still resentment, righteous anger is still anger. As long as we believe there can be appropriate anger, appropriate resentment, appropriate jealousy or an appropriate version of any inappropriate quality, we create an inappropriate situation, anger and resentment can never be justified. This does not mean we cannot respond to situations, it means that anger and resentment can never be justified.

Can we act appropriately when we have been victimized? In some situations the aggressor, the abuser, thinks he is a victim, and since he believes he is the victim he thinks his actions are a necessary response, appropriate protection of the victim. By protecting the baby inside himself he becomes a terrible creature, a powerful abuser. Some of the greatest tyrants in the world thought of themselves as victims. They say many of Hitler's actions came from this sense of victimhood. When we believe ourselves to be a victim we can grant ourselves license to do terrible things, we allow certain things because we are a victim. Although there are situations in which we are, in fact, a victim, it is dangerous to identify ourselves that way. What we take personally and cannot let go of causes more harm than anything done to us, we damage our inner self. In the end it is all about our inner self, about who we are, who we become, the way we act, the way we react, why we react, our qualities.

Does this mean we cannot tell someone that what he is doing is wrong? Of course we can, but can we do it without being angry, without thinking of ourselves as a victim? Can we understand that people behave as their own nature prompts, and not because of us? So many people take everything personally, yet almost nothing is. People try to rectify what they think is happening in their life, to make it manageable for their understanding they push and pull everything around them. If we are in their way we are in trouble, we do need to stay away from certain people, keep away from the web certain people weave. We have to watch and be careful, but we should also understand that appropriate action can be taken without emotional baggage. This baggage is our own problem, a problem which keeps us from peace. It becomes a dark undercurrent of inner, illusory influences which keep finding ways to destroy our peace, making us blame someone or something else for our problems, making us angry, refusing to accept our situation. These forces of darkness and illusion only need to keep us dissatisfied to accomplish their mission.

Our mission is to learn how to be satisfied, to be grateful enough to say, "O my God, you have given me more than enough." We have all been in that place of gratitude, that place of acceptance we sometimes fall into. We have to learn how to stay there, how to go from a state to a station, from glimpses to reality itself. Rather than stepping in and out, in and out, we should know how to open the door, cross the threshold and move on instead of hovering somewhere in between. We initiate this movement with the help of God's grace, but we stop ourselves from proceeding, no one else does.

Our inner network of baser qualities stops us, and we do have base, lower qualities, the dark forces living with us which we need to bind and ignore. We need to be rid of them, not let them impose themselves on our true consciousness, then we can have peace. If we have the faith that the right thing happens at the right time, there is peace; if we have the conviction that God's plan is right, there is peace. We cannot say, "God, this is the way it's going to be, I'm taking You on." We cannot fight with God, it is not a fight we can win. Only elemental turmoil and an association with inappropriate forces project a fight like that.

Usually, we associate with illusion instead of associating with God. As we learn how to associate correctly with what is appropriate, our inner action simultaneously disconnects us from the inappropriate. When we get better at this we are satisfied to sit in the sun when we are sitting in the sun, we are satisfied to sit in the shade when we are sitting in the shade. If we notice that wherever we find ourselves we want to be somewhere else, whatever we find ourselves doing we want to be doing something else, whatever situation we find ourselves in we want a different situation, this means we have not found peace, we have no rest because we have not understood where we need to be.

When we discover we are fighting with ourselves it helps us stop the fight, but first we have to make that discovery. People can be caught up in a chase all their life and never catch up to anything, never understand why they chase what they are pursuing. This becomes their life, then of course, if they should hold what they have chased in their hands they do not know what to do with it, and they chase the next thing. Every once in awhile when these desires, these needs, are fulfilled we see how meaningless they are, we understand that what drives us is desire, not the object we think we need. The world says the journey is in the chase, it has meaning, it has truth, but this is a deception making us believe there is some benefit in conflict, some benefit in all the pushing and pulling. Whenever we listen to what the world says we continue the chase. We need to slow down, stop and ask ourselves where am I, who am I, what is the truth about myself? Such moments of recognition are moments of opportunity, we enter a place between levels of consciousness which can take us to a higher level where we can see that our thoughts are irrelevant, our desires are irrelevant, our conflicts are irrelevant, that our life is filled with petty things.

This recognition is a gift, as we reduce the importance of those things in our life we usually give importance, to we can begin to understand humility, we can give greater importance to inner peace, something which changes us. Who we are begins to change, our life begins to change, we interact differently, we respond differently to criticism and blame, we are not as attached to the things which used to control us.

We can make an egocentric do almost anything by praising him; if we blame him he might kill us. We all have so many triggers pushing us to respond a certain way. When we know our triggers, find out what sets us off, what makes us do the things we do then center ourselves in God's grace instead, we can change. May we discover our capacity for this change.

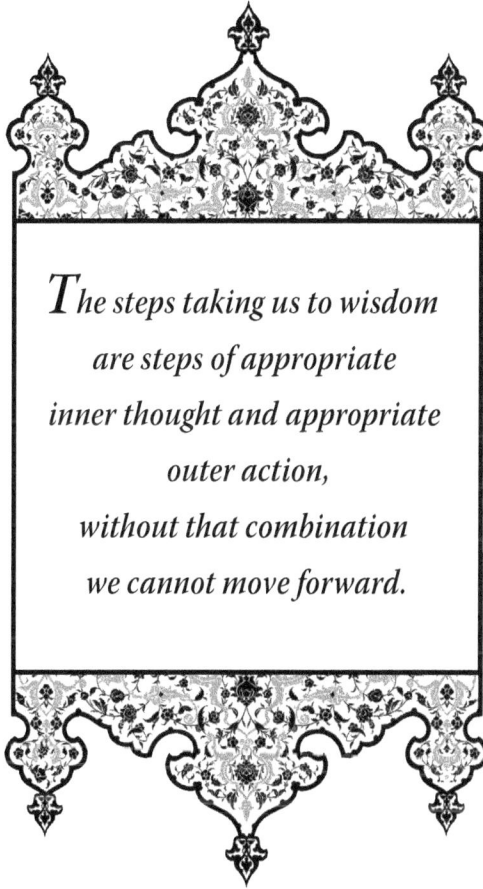

*The steps taking us to wisdom
are steps of appropriate
inner thought and appropriate
outer action,
without that combination
we cannot move forward.*

CHAPTER SIX

The Requisites of Wisdom

Without being able to add and subtract it is unlikely we can multiply. There is a certain progression in most things necessary to move forward, but quite often either ignorance or arrogance stands in our way; together they can take us to places where angels fear to tread. We should be able to acknowledge the limits of the knowledge we have and know how far it can take us. A most important thing to recognize is what we do not know, if we are content with what we already know, there is no reason to move along. A recent book explained we cannot go into business without knowing algebra because business deals with unknowns, with assumptions that project them into the future. If we cannot do this we cannot develop a business, if we are ignorant about numbers and how they work, unaware we are supposed to buy low and sell high, we will have difficulty.

There is a story about a man who bought watermelons in a farming community which he took for sale to the city. He bought a truck, bought five hundred watermelons, as much as his truck could hold, for a dollar each at the farm. He took them to the city, selling them all immediately for a dollar each. He was so successful he made three trips a day, but at the end of the week he realized he had not made any money. He talked this over with his wife and they decided he needed a bigger truck. This is the way of ignorance, we keep looking for bigger trucks, looking for solutions which have nothing to do with the problem confronting us. Until we analyze a situation correctly there are no solutions, there is nothing but the sorrow of covering the same ground again and again.

How do we understand what wisdom is, how do we learn what genuine analysis is? To begin with, we need to understand the requisites of a specific state. Just as we cannot multiply when we cannot add and subtract, how are we to be wise when we cannot hold our tongue? If we cannot listen, how can we possibly understand what someone is trying to say? When our mind is so busy reacting, how are we to accept what is offered? If our own pain is overwhelming, how can we empathize with the pain of others? If our own hunger is overwhelming, how can we feel the hunger of others? If our own needs are incapacitating, how can we possibly feel the needs of others?

What drives us? This should be our first question, what pushes us, in which direction, where are we taking ourselves? If we took the train to Boston it will not take us to Washington, it is not more complicated than that, and yet we fail to consult the maps, we do not hear the conductor announcing which way we are going, and when we arrive in Boston we are surprised not to be in Washington. When ignorance combines with arrogance this can happen, when we push ourselves along without appropriate training or knowledge, a refusal to admit what we do not know, this happens, not only to individuals but to whole societies as well.

Much of science is based on false assumptions. In conjunction with the arrogance of many scientists, this can produce solutions which become accepted theories until they are proved wrong. Recently, the newspapers had stories that the Milky Way is about twice as big as scientists always thought it was. Until a few days ago the scientific community was convinced the Milky Way was half its size; soon there might be a different assumption. Scientists tend to be profoundly assertive with assumptions and theories, as well as profoundly assertive with reasons for change. Facts change, but arrogance does not.

If we ourselves are to change, something must happen to our arrogance. By doing away with arrogance we can begin to attack ignorance, we cannot do one without the other. We need to admit we do not know, learn how to deal correctly with not knowing. We need to find people who know specific things, stay with such people so that we can learn. Once when I was City Solicitor I needed answers to some questions on municipal law. I called the author of several books on this subject and asked if he would mind talking to me. "Mind?" he said, "I'm seventy-two years old and nobody talks to me, I would love to talk to you." This saved me a lot of time and made it possible for me to respond to complex situations with authority.

We should learn how to do this for the complex situations we encounter, we should understand what we know and what we have to do, then learn appropriate methods. Without an appropriate method we repeat the same mistakes again and again, we keep guessing. A young man who was dyslexic and not doing well in school thought it was because he could not guess as well as everyone else. With his reading difficulty, studying before an exam was unknown to him, he made different assumptions. Until he understood his problem he could not resolve it on his own.

We all have problems we cannot resolve on our own, but we have someone to help us, and we should develop a connection to that source. God is waiting for us to walk through the open door, yet all we do is knock. We have to change our approach, acknowledge our inability, admit we know there is a source of power just waiting to help us, a power so great it can resolve everything. The mercy of this power is transforming, the compassion of this power is beyond our ability to comprehend, and it is there for us. We were created by it, that power is our Father who will treat us as His child.

We need to believe this, our belief alone lets us walk through the open door, or else we just keep knocking. If we think we belong we walk in. What is the level of comfort with our Father, the Creator of the universe? What is our attitude and our state of awe? Do we compare ourselves to Him, or do we realize He is all that exists, the point of our life is to be one with Him? Do we realize the nature of our existence correctly, do we have assumptions about the nature of existence, assumptions which either hold us in place or let us expand? Our assumptions hold us in place as a separate entity, or they let us dissolve within the glory of reality. We need to discover whether our powerful assumptions about existence are appropriate or not, remembering always that we have been taught by people who do not themselves know. We have acquired their ideas of no value, we think in their inappropriate ways.

We must acquire appropriate thoughts, appropriate ideas, an appropriate system of beliefs, but that is not enough. We can say we believe in God, the prophets, the angels and Judgment Day, but do we really believe in them, do we live as if God is watching us, as if we are in contact with reality, with God? Or do we divide our life into segments, times when God cannot see us and times when He can, times when we do not see ourselves and times when we do? When a cat drinks milk it closes its eyes and thinks no one can see it. This is a common human condition, people walk around with their minds and hearts shut thinking no one can see them.

When we begin to understand things like this, incorporating the understanding into each moment of existence, we begin to understand the steps which will take us to wisdom. The steps taking us to wisdom are steps of appropriate inner thought and appropriate outer action, without that combination we cannot move forward. If our thoughts are filled with lust how can we move to a higher consciousness? If our thoughts are filled with greed how can we move to a higher consciousness? If our thoughts are filled with jealousy how can we move to a higher consciousness? If we have thoughts of resentment or hate how can we move to a higher consciousness? Truth will not live in these obstacles, we need to move to a place where reality exists, move there with our whole being, then everything changes, we attract different things, we spend time with different people. Those who are not walking His way are like thorns, and just as we avoid walking on thorns we avoid them too, we understand what they do.

We do not juggle knives without being cut, we can see this is foolish to try, but there is foolish behavior we are unaware of. We are unaware of the scars in our consciousness greed imposes, unaware of the scars in our consciousness resentment imposes, we are unaware of the damage ill will imposes. We think ill will towards others punishes them, but the container holds the acid. The container of our being is damaged by the acids of jealousy, resentment, hatred, they are the acids which eat us.

We cannot allow ourselves to be eaten, we have to be rid of these things, replace them with things which repair and heal. Love heals the scars of mistreatment, love heals the abuse we have received. We should learn how to love ourselves, how to love others, learn how to forgive the abusers and the abuse. This is the way to be healed. Without forgiveness the acid is not removed, it is still there. Forgiveness is the alchemy changing the acid we carry around, forgiveness stops the burning and starts the healing. We have to go through this change, this process of changing acid to love, then our relations with the world change. As the world becomes less and less meaningful to us we turn to the reality of existence, we find the understanding of a secret transformation. We must pray that God aids us in this transformation and allows this healing transformation to occur.

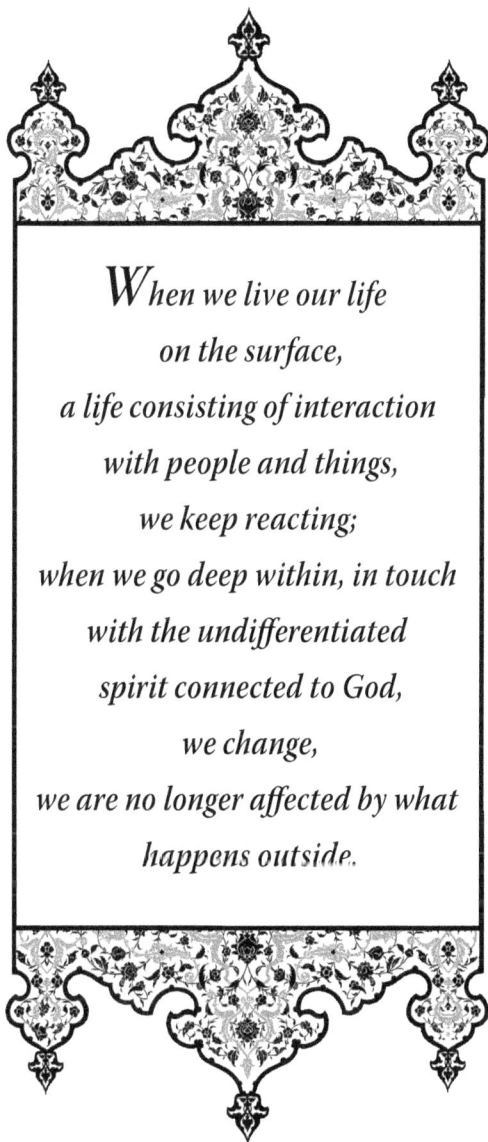

CHAPTER SEVEN

*When we live our life
on the surface,
a life consisting of interaction
with people and things,
we keep reacting;
when we go deep within, in touch
with the undifferentiated
spirit connected to God,
we change,
we are no longer affected by what
happens outside.*

The Life Within

Much of what needs to be clarified in our life is the difference between living in illusion and living in reality. We find many things difficult, many things we cannot avoid are difficult for us. Some situations cause anxiety, others cause fear. There is so much fear in the world. Some people are afraid to leave their house, some are afraid to go to work, others are afraid they will be fired. People fear what will happen tomorrow, they worry about their sustenance, maintaining themselves and their families.

When we consider the state of the world and everything happening all around, fear is understandable. The explosive disasters in places across the world over the last few years are enough to account for certain kinds of fear. Some people also bring fear to their relationships. Fear is not uncommon, although it does belong to the world of illusion, it is part of illusion, but certain wise people have said that when we exist in truth, we are beyond hope and beyond fear. This seems to be contradictory—what it means is that truth is so overwhelming, so beyond our conception in the way we think now, that once we understand God's immensity, His greatness and His reality, the truth is so transforming that the way we now think about things disappears in this level of understanding.

Some people of wisdom have been called sons of the moment because they live in this instant, they are grateful for this instant, they are engaged in this instant. When we are involved in this moment, this instant, there is no place for fear which is attached to the future. Fear is connected to events which might occur in the future or what might have happened in the past. We conclude in advance how things will occur, before we know how circumstances will unfold. By not living in the moment, by not living right now, we live in illusion, we live in our mind, in that space where our imagination creates what will occur. We live in the movie of our life instead of the moment of our life; as long as we live in the movie of our life we are not connected to the reality which exists only in this moment. There is no past, there is no future, there is only now. If we are lost to the now we are lost to reality, we merely look at our life imagining who we are with that part of us which sees from the outside, which examines our life from the outside. How do we spend our time, what do we think about? Are we caught up in what we think will happen next or are we actually living now?

God is closer to us then our jugular vein, not tomorrow, now. God re-creates us with every breath. When does that breath occur? It occurs now. If we are thinking about a situation which will manifest three days from now, we are presupposing reality instead of living it; we should stop supposing and start living. We do not exist in the past and we do not exist in the future, we exist now. When we are in that now we can be grateful for what exists now, we breathe now, we are conscious of God now, we are sustained by Him now, and now we can study every manifest thing He created as lessons about Himself. When we live in this moment, in the now, the mind slows down. If it does not have future or past to think about, what is there to occupy it?

Just like any other ocean, the ocean of illusion becomes still only when we dive very deep, our focus must be deep and powerful. The waves on the surface of the ocean are in constant motion, affected by everything, a passing boat, the winds that blow, but when we go deep below there is a stillness. When we live our life on the surface, a life consisting of interaction with people and things, we keep reacting; when we go deep within, in touch with the undifferentiated spirit connected to God, we change, we are no longer affected by what happens outside.

We can look at an ocean from the sky or from a submarine and see two different things, it is the same ocean but our perspective has changed. We need to submerge like a submarine, submerge within ourselves. This is a way to stop subjecting ourselves to all the irritations of the world, to stop subjecting ourselves to all the pushes and pulls of everything we come into contact with. If we are centered at our core we react from the inside, not in response to what is going on outside. This means a change of focus in our approach to the world: as long as the world is important to us, as long as we fear losing any of it, not only do we fear losing what we have, we also fear not getting what we want.

Fear is connected to our attachment to the world. Once we lose that attachment we lose our fear. Hope is attached to what we have, what we want to do with what we have, what we hope to get from the world. Fear and hope are both attached to the world, but grace and glory are attached to God, divine radiance is attached to God, wisdom is attached to God, compassion, mercy, generosity and greatness are attached to God.

We need to make a choice, choose whether we are attached to uncertain hope, to fear and the things of the world, or whether we are attached to God. If we are attached to the world all the things that come with that attachment will tag along, anxiety, depression, exuberance. Everything that happens in psychotic states can also, to an extent, accompany wanting, losing and getting the world. Reactions are determined by how much we get and how much we lose, we keep score, how much did I get today, how much did I lose today, what are my possibilities for getting and losing in the future?

We use the world to keep score. Once we stop keeping score this way, once gratification comes from a different place, we change. Nevertheless, as long as we have that attachment to what we get and what we lose, we are locked onto fear and hope, we cannot be at peace. It is the way of the world, things are constantly being given and taken, things are created and destroyed, a never-ending process, continuing turmoil. Give, take, create, destroy, destruction, rebirth, it does not stop. If we are involved in the process and attached to it, we become emotional seesaws pulled up and down by that process.

Living things are described by science as irritable, if we prod a one-celled animal like an amoeba with a pin, it moves, it is irritable. If we prod a stone with a pin, it does not move. In a broad sense this describes our life, we are irritated by our surroundings, we are irritated in a joyful way or a depressed way, in a happy way or a sad way. We think these states are different, but from a broader perspective they can be seen as mere reactions to the world, we react to the world and give different names to our reactions. Not only do we give different names to different reactions, we also classify them as good and bad, right and wrong. If I win it is right, if you win it is wrong. This is the way we think, the way we integrate ourselves with the world, and it is something we need to disengage, we need to be free of this worldly play.

Some of us watch soap operas, some of us live soap operas. Whether we watch it on television or live it, it is the same thing. If we take our satisfaction from the unending interactions of the world, this means we are sustained by drama, and there is so much drama in the world. If we want political drama we have political drama, enthusiasm for our candidate and anger at his opponent. If we want show business or entertainment drama there is so much of that, daily programs about rising stars and fading stars—interesting that we describe people as celestial bodies. If we want financial drama, there is the stock market.

The ability to withdraw from this game, withdraw from the drama, means we need to alter ourselves. We have lived the drama for so long we believe it is our life, we have measured ourselves by its rules for so long we believe we are measured by how successful or unsuccessful we are in the dramas of the world. God's rules are different, we have to make only one decision, do we want to live our life according to the world's rules or God's rules, do we wish to master illusion or surrender to God?

Imagine conquering illusion. History is full of the men who tried to conquer illusion, they defined what they wanted to conquer and some did. Yet they have all disappeared, none of them exist any longer, they are all chapters in a history book, a chapter which becomes smaller and smaller as times goes by. History seems to pay more attention to what happened recently than to what happened in the past. The story of our own life exists for a very small moment in time, either we live our life or we live the drama. We should decide which we want.

If our life is dedicated to the show in front of us, being entertained by the drama, being involved in the drama, we have missed the point of existence. We must refocus this point, a nonstop endeavor; when we are not focused we are caught in the drama, we are actors who have lost touch with their true selves, we have become the character we play. Method acting is taught this way, they teach actors to lose themselves and become the character they play. In our own life we create the character we become, forgetting who we really are. We are so good at this everyone recognizes us as the character we play, we use that name, we do what is expected of this character in every situation. We have lost the ability to go out of character, we are stuck in a caricature, we become caricatures of true human beings as we attempt to fit into the drama of the world and play by its rules.

Why does this happen? We have been caught up in the praise and blame which affect our life, we walk through life searching for praise. When someone says 'good' we do more of that, when someone says 'bad' we stop doing that. Words of praise and blame are directed at us from the time we are children. What we learn as children is written on stone, and so if we are addicted to praise and run from blame, we will continue to run from blame and search for praise until we can stop, until we realize what others say does not matter because what matters is the way God sees us. It does not matter what the community thinks as long as we do what we know to be right. If we do not know what is right we should find someone who does, find the fragrance of what is correct and go towards it, find the taste of what is correct and go towards it.

God has been good to us, placing people in the world who know what is correct, what is not, sending books telling us what is correct, what is not, and every once in awhile, a teacher who knows. We need to learn how to listen to these people, learn how to understand what they are saying. If they happen to be outside the mainstream, perhaps we should become a small tributary. Everyone jumps into the river of the world, the same stream. We have to get away from that stream and find our own way, find the way to God, something we can do only if we go deep inside ourselves, break our attachments to the world. The world is a fishhook, once it is cast and goes into us, wherever it pulls we have to go. The primary hook penetrates us and a small barb makes it difficult to pull out.

We have learned right and wrong in a worldly context for so long, we are so addicted to what we believe is right, what we believe is wrong, it has become difficult for us to change. This is like pulling the barb of the fishhook out, we have to go through the pain of giving up everything we thought was correct, everything we have held onto as correct for so long. It means we have to go through the pain of recognizing we have been misled, that we have also misled others.

We have been on both sides of the equation, spouting the world as if it were true, living the world as if it were true, and we have taken other people along with us on the wrong path. Whenever we have to give up something we valued, we mourn the passing of the thing which was our foundation for so long. How can we just give it up? Consult the obituary pages, they tell us that whether we decide to give it up or not, it will be given up.

When will the giving up happen? Will it all be pulled out from under us, or will there be a time when we surrender to reality, whether we are ready or not? If we die before death what are we dying to? We die to the world, dying to the world is the way we conclude our experience of the world. This small death must occur before the larger death; be aware of it, be joyous in it.

The more we give up the more we get, this is what we need to understand. Knowing unity does not mean giving anything up, it means becoming part of the treasure allotted to us, entering the glory, becoming part of the divine radiance beyond imagination. When we are one with the truth, fear and hope both disappear because they are irrelevant, there is no place for fear and hope. May God grant us this, may He open our heart so that fear leaves, so that desire leaves, so that our attachments leave and we understand His true glory.

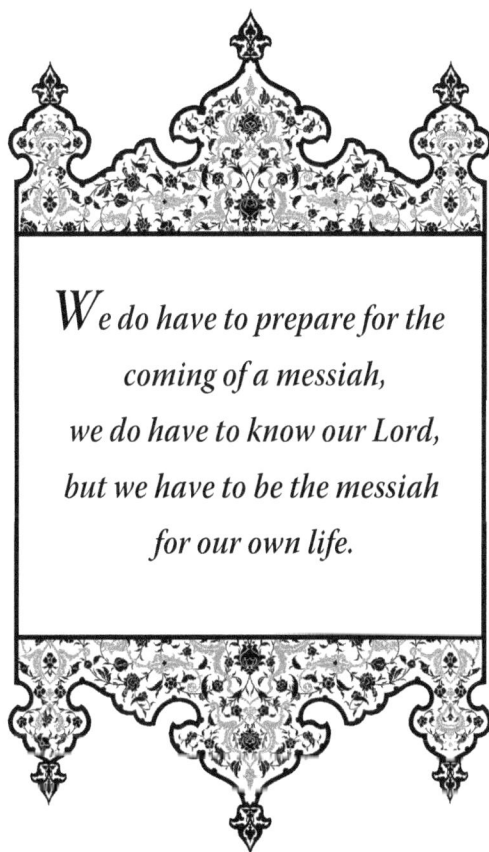

*We do have to prepare for the
coming of a messiah,
we do have to know our Lord,
but we have to be the messiah
for our own life.*

Saving the World

Scripture tells us that if we kill one man we have destroyed all mankind, if we save one man we have saved all mankind. We have been told that God created man as the culmination of all His creation, that when He created man He rolled the universe into a ball and placed it in the heart of each man. Who is man, what is man, what is his purpose? Man is the highest of God's creation holding the secrets of the universe, the secret of our Creator. We have been told again and again, if we know ourselves we will know our Creator. What are we trying to know, what are we trying to accomplish? We seem to have replaced the search for an understanding of ourselves with the search for an understanding of the world, we have made interaction with the world our priority.

As long as the world is our priority we have lost our focus, we have lost the purpose of our creation, to know God. As we know the world better and better, as we interact more and more with it we assume we can change it, the understanding that God's will controls the world is lost. He is the creator, the sustainer and nourisher. If He were to stop sustaining the world for an instant what would happen? But we continue to act as though our effort sustains the world, as though our effort keeps the world peaceful, our ability to control the elements holds off the end. Governments act as if they held the key to peace because we believe that is true.

What is the strength of one man who knows his God, his Lord, and what is the strength of that truth manifest in the world? What happens when one person is so in tune with his Creator that He is revealed, manifest in that person's ability to be one with God? We are told creation exists so that God can experience the world through someone who experiences Him. If that is lost, if that person who knows his Lord is lost to the world there is no longer any reason for creation. This world was created for us to know God.

Each of the monotheist religions talks of a coming messiah, they believe in a messiah. Christianity believes Jesus will return, Islam believes the mahdī will come, in Judaism some believe the messiah has come, some believe he will come. We must know who the messiah is for our life, know what our connection to that messiah should be. If we have the entire universe within us we have the messiah there too. If the messiah is to come, will he come through someone else, are we not all one, is there not oneness in creation? We do have to prepare for the coming of a messiah, we do have to know our Lord, but we have to be the messiah for our own life. We save our own life by being that messiah, and this implies that all mankind is saved.

This is the work of the Sufi path, of those who walk the path to reality. Railing against the world means a descent from our higher to our lower self because we bring all our animal instincts to the world and act with them. This is what we chronicle, our animal actions, a level of action we call our history, this is what our history books record.

It would be good to produce a generation of human beings who act as human beings. This is difficult as long as the world refuses to accept there is such a thing as a true human being, as long as the world refuses to accept we are the culmination of God's creation. The world says we have descended from the ape, or more specifically, some have said from the baboon because the ape is not aggressive enough. If they keep telling us we are the descendent of a baboon, what can we aspire to? Although much of the world lives in the state of a baboon, we must understand we are more than that and reject this definition. We define the world, it does not define us.

Because some lie to us about who and what we are does not

mean we accept the lie. Accepting the lie means accepting that we live on an island without knowing how to swim, accepting there is no escape, we are trapped, this life is the beginning and end of existence. It is not true, we can swim, we can fly, we are not what the world defines, we are not our lower self. We should find people who have realized this and gather around them to learn how to be like them. The only way to save the world is by becoming what we are supposed to be, by acquiring the qualities of our Creator. To learn these qualities we need to find mirrors who reflect them, the people who reflect them, the people who are these qualities. When we are connected to a true human being we can become a true human being, we can unlearn the inappropriate things we have accepted and discover new truths about existence, the truth of who we are.

The lower self has been at war with God since the beginning of time, the forces of darkness and illusion in the form of satan have been at war with God since the beginning of time. This war has been fought to convince us we have no real relationship with God, we are lesser beings, this is a war which began when satan refused to bow down before man. Since then he has been trying to prove his refusal was appropriate, that God was wrong. This is our battle: was God wrong, was satan right? Who are we, what do we prove? We should understand our true nature and learn how to spend more time in a higher state, in our higher self. We know the difference between our elevated, transcendent state and a lower state, we know what pulls at us in that lower state. We need to discover how to stay in a transcendent state for periods of time, it must be our inner work which we cannot accomplish by changing someone else, by fighting with others or talking about creating utopian societies. We do this work one person at a time, one heart at a time. If it works on our own heart it can work on others, one heart expanding in the vibration of truth.

We should understand our place in existence. This is what enlightened beings have been trying to teach, reality, not the business of the world. We are a function of God's supreme grace independent of nation, religion or race. When we recognize that the whole universe exists in one heart we no longer use a definition of the world which denies our true state. We exist at the center, not as a soul apart. When we are centered in the boundless glory of God's own might, God manifests as we fulfill His request. May He make this quest our intention and may this intention be fulfilled.

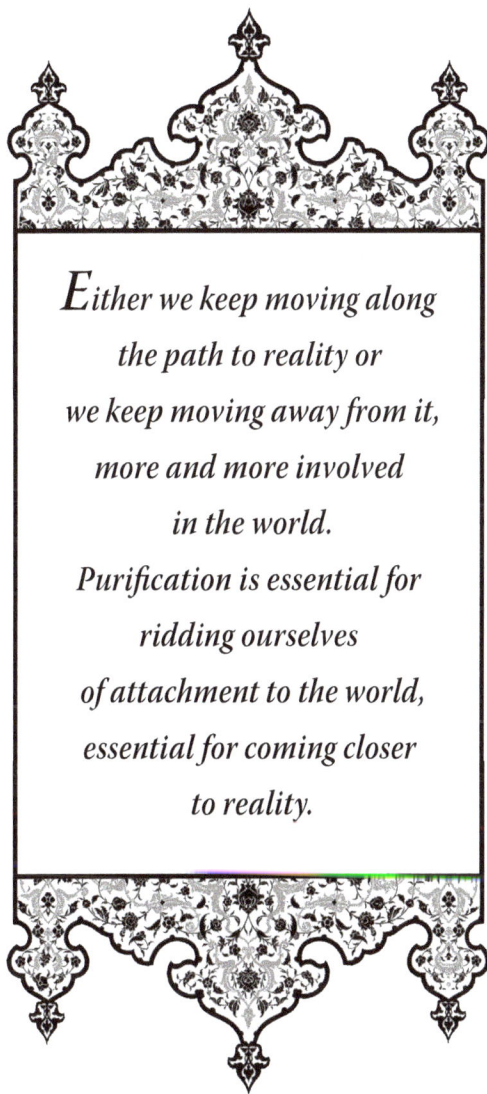

*Either we keep moving along
the path to reality or
we keep moving away from it,
more and more involved
in the world.
Purification is essential for
ridding ourselves
of attachment to the world,
essential for coming closer
to reality.*

Handling Illusion

Either we keep moving along the path to reality or we keep moving away from it, more and more involved in the world. Purification is essential for ridding ourselves of attachment to the world, essential for coming closer to reality. Because God allows things of no value, sometimes when we look at the world we value things incorrectly, we assign them a value they do not have and react as if they had. If we think something is important we protect it, we fight for it because it is important, otherwise we might let it go, prepared to treat it casually, without respect, even shabbily.

To examine where we are on this path we need to consider how we treat certain things of the world. Do we respect money, power, expensive things, do we respect prayer and solitude? When we arrive in a city where there is little excitement, do we say there is nothing here? In the desert, in places where prophets had revelations, we could say there is nothing to do, right there in those places where prophets had the universe revealed to them. Understand what nothing means, understand the importance of nothing. When the world becomes small, at that point we begin to discover the unseen. Our lower self, our base desires will always vote for illusion, for darkness, they will always proclaim whatever is inappropriate and wrong as truth. They do this consistently; we should never underestimate the strength and arrogance of our baser side, nor should we try to gauge someone else's.

Every inappropriate thing begins with pride—the first major dispute in the history of the world came up when satan refused to bow to Adam. He thought Adam was inferior, less than he was. God told him he was to bow down, but satan insisted he would pray anywhere to God, but not behind Adam. That rationalization meant he wanted to pray, except he thought God was wrong, he wanted to do what God commanded, except that God was wrong. These rationalizations of 'but' and 'except' are all enemies of surrender. Without truly understanding surrender it is easy to rationalize, an available trap. Our baser self will not confess to disputing with God, it will not realize that is what we are doing, it will just think what we are told is inappropriate, incorrect.

These are the tactics of darkness and illusion, they instill doubt, they make us wonder about our fate, wonder about what the prophets said. Doubt initiates all this distress, but if we put this doubt aside, box it and contain it by recognizing it for what it is, it will not interfere with our thoughts, we have handled it. If we let it out of that box it will shake us to our roots. Our base desires do not leave us, we spend our life with them, and that means we need to develop a method, a way to live with them. The method involves not paying attention to them. Once we understand their characteristics, once we understand how they work and their relentless nature, we learn they will not stop. If we know this we can accept they are something else, not who we are, but if we are confused, thinking they are part of who we are, it is difficult to keep them in check.

Our quest for reality and purification means disengaging fantasy, disengaging imagination, yet today computers offer worlds of fantasy we can step into, worlds which take us further and further from reality. These fantasy worlds have become an addictive reality for many who try to escape from illusion by going deeper into illusion. Some of us do recognize the problems people have with illusory worlds, problems for which they actually seek a cure. Unfortunately, the world is full of cures which do not work, cures which only bring deeper trouble. The truth has been offered, it has been shown to us, it is only a question of whether or not we accept it. What about those who have not seen this truth, this reality, do we not have a responsibility to the few we know, should we not let them know we have found a path which is true? Should we not offer it to them, help them find a cure for the troubles in their illusory worlds?

That would be charity, if a smile can be charity, how much greater is the charity of love, how much greater is the charity which brings truth to those who do not understand God? What more can we do than offer the truth, offer an opportunity to choose? Those who have an inkling of truth should make an effort to bring it to others, something we do with our qualities. When we stay calm and peaceful in the midst of turmoil, others will ask how we do it, and that gives us the opportunity to offer truth. Most people do not understand how lost they are until a crisis shows them that parts of their existence do not make sense, that something is missing, there is a hole in their consciousness, an emptiness which needs to be filled. This is a moment when we can do something, those who are on the path of love have an obligation to do this, to manifest love so that people can see what must be seen. We have an obligation to pass this along, it is not supposed to stop with us.

God has told us He is merciful, He is always merciful. If He withdrew from this world it would disappear, but He maintains and sustains us. With each breath we are proof of His maintaining and sustenance, each breath should recognize that. If our consciousness follows our breath there is no room for doubt, as we breathe we acknowledge the existence of the sustainer, each breath an opportunity to affirm our faith. Each time we do not make the affirmation, the opportunity which never comes again, that breath is gone without acknowledging our gratitude.

What do we lose? We are given the capacity to experience gratitude, a gift allowing us to taste one of God's qualities. He is gratitude, when we experience gratitude we are gratitude. Each moment we fail to breathe our acknowledgment of His sustenance we lose the opportunity. God does not lose anything when we do not praise Him, but we lose, the reality of our existence lies in that praise, that acknowledgment. When we are busy doing other things we miss the opportunity to praise Him, we are lost, distracted, pulled towards everything unreal until we turn to reality again. The next breath is another opportunity to acknowledge Him, that is God's mercy, each breath gives us an opportunity to find reality, to acknowledge Him, affirming the existence which alone makes ours possible.

Our existence is tied to Him, enmeshed in Him, He is all there is. In that acknowledgment, as we disappear, there is a glory beyond understanding. The world tells us if we give our self up for Him we lose our self, but that is the point, reality opens only when we lose our self. When we are on the wrong side of this, we are lost in the self, lost in some great problem, illusion, the enemy of our state, the enemy of reality. The world turns everything upside down, everything has been turned around and lied about, lies we repeat as our reality. We have to spend time ridding ourselves of the lies we have been taught, then we can act appropriately, then we can believe appropriately, understand appropriately. There is so much which is either inappropriate or useless, so much we call knowledge which confers a title, and our baser self is certainly interested in titles. Where will that title take us, what will it do for us? We do have to make a living, we must do something in the world, work for what we need, yet we also have to work for what our soul needs. We have to do both simultaneously.

God has no body, no illness or aging, He does not need food, He has no children, no family, none of the things we have an obligation to deal with. Because we do have all this we are caught between two worlds, this world and the next. That means we have to center ourselves, something requiring great patience, an inner peace which disposes of anxiety, an attitude which does not respond to difficulties by retaliating. When we are not aggressive no matter the commotion all around us, there is inner peace. What is this, how does it happen, why does it happen, who are we when it happens?

Recognize that one of the states we have is peace. How do we bring ourselves back to that place of peace although we keep flying away from it, we keep flying away and coming back. Regular prayer is a simple reminder that even if we have our daily work, our daily duties, the time we need for the world, we also make time for devotion to God, for peace with Him. The opportunity for prayer exists with every breath. Can we do that, take our devotion to the next level so that it is automatically part of our existence? In that state, as we take care of tasks in the world, our devotion continues without stopping, our attitude and our actions remain appropriate. Now our conscience guides us, His will guides us if we give up attachment to stay in that place of praise.

This means change, taking ourselves to another state, the state of all the holy beings who do their duty to each person they see. How can their attention be fixed on each person they see yet be entirely with God? They are not there, God does it all while they surrender in praise of Him. They do God's work as He maintains, sustains and protects. These holy beings assist with God's work. When we see those who work only on behalf of others, we witness God's work as it manifests in human beings, a strong presence, powerful, it shakes us. A vibration goes through us when we see it alive, manifest, walking among us.

This gift of God is like air, it is here for everyone, it is everywhere. We have to breathe to get the air, if we hold our breath too long we die. If we keep resisting God's gifts we could die before we recognize them. We should stop resisting, we do stop holding our breath because it hurts in the end. As we resist the understanding that He alone exists we hurt ourselves. Understand the truth and give up the lies we have been told. Surrender is the greatest treasure, we lose and gain everything. May we accept this gift.

Trying to find our identity,
trying to discover
who we are,
this is the core of the
mystical journey.

Domesticating Our Animal Qualities

Trying to find our identity, trying to discover who we are, this is the core of the mystical journey. To understand who we are we need to understand who we are not—some of the misery, confusion and sadness we might encounter on this path comes from the confusion between who we are and who we are not. There is a traditional gnostic understanding that human beings have two aspects, two driving forces, one is the lower part, the animal self, the other is the soul connected to God. The animal self takes care of our needs in this world, carrying out tasks which provide for us physically. All the animals do the same things, they find shelter, they procreate, they understand how to find food in the same way that we, as physical beings, do what the animals do.

Animals have specific qualities we recognize by characterizing them as the sly fox, the graceful swan, the shy deer. Within the same species, the animals all function similarly, they do the same things in the same way, again and again. The size and weight of an elephant will always let it push where it wants to go, pushing things out of the way instead of going around them. Elephants clear paths through the jungle which other animals can use, they are helpful for that, but they do push their way through. All the different kinds of deer are frightened by the slightest sound, they all run away.

Everything in creation exists within us, the attributes of each animal exist within us too. To what extent do we have their qualities, when do they dominate our consciousness, when are we like an elephant pushing things out of our way, when are we like a deer, frightened and running away? These are the differing poles of our behavior which sometimes make it difficult to be in the right inner state as we approach the world. If we are demolishing a house we need the qualities of an elephant, a positive thing, in a war zone we might need the qualities of a deer to escape, we know we should be afraid, but if we act like an elephant in front of a tank the consequences are disastrous.

A problem arises if we think of ourselves and identify ourselves with the aspects of the self we use in the material world, then we think of who we are, we identify ourselves as animal. Certain animal operations give us things we like: other animals are afraid of elephants, and so if we are good at being an elephant we cause fear, and with fear comes respect. We might like that persona, we might like the elephant. If we amass enough we discover the power in money, provide for our family like a female lion bringing back the food.

With these qualities we acquire respect and status in the physical world. The more we identify ourselves with animal qualities, the more they dominate, but the problem of their limitations remain, they cannot transcend the illusion which is the world they were made to function in. We have to acknowledge the material side of ourselves, our physical side, the animal side, yet if we confer reality on that we are limited to a life of illusion without any possibility of its transcendence.

These animal qualities are subservient to certain principles of natural law, principles which mean doing whatever is necessary to achieve the desired end. If a lion wants to eat it jumps on another creature and destroys it; the lion in us does the same thing. If a fox wants something it will steal; if we use the qualities of a fox we do the same thing. When we are dominated by our animal qualities we place ourselves beyond restriction. The prophets came to teach us restriction with the understanding that although we need to function in the physical realm, we should function there within the boundaries that keep us from descending to the animal way of doing things.

Animal qualities do not normally recognize boundaries unless we train them, just as we domesticate the animals themselves, but some animals cannot be domesticated, and such an animal is of no use to us. We should only function in the physical realm to maintain ourselves, fulfilling our physical needs. It is dangerous to allow the animal side to be in control, dangerous to make our animal nature important, or to think of it as something majestic, something beautiful and soaring. We should know the limits of our animal nature, and know that we must not identify ourselves with it. Animals are wild, without restraint. Without domesticating or training the animals inside us to be obedient to spiritual demands, we are subject to their wildness.

When we intend to take a spiritual path, to rise above the world of illusion, we cannot identify ourselves with illusion or anything dealing with illusion. Everything we see, everything we touch, everything we engage with our senses has a time span, a duration, all that will disappear. Once we identify ourselves with something that disappears our life is identified with the temporary. To identify ourselves with the permanent we have to live beyond illusion, in the world of the permanent. This permanence is not seen by our physical eyes, it cannot be smelled by our nose, or even touched by any of our senses. This is the world of the soul, a different world which requires a different identification to enter.

The tea we drink has a certain taste we did nothing to create, nor did we create our sense of taste. The flavor, the taste, is inherent in the tea or in whatever we eat. God is inherent in everything in the same way, but can we taste it, can we go to the place where we can savor that taste? When we want to taste a mango we have to find one and eat it, but God alone can put God in our mouth, in our heart, He can give us His taste as He wills. There is a teaching tradition which reminds us to trust in God but tie up our camel as well. Among the many things this means, we are to understand we must try to find God ourselves, we must make an effort to find the truth, to find the reality which exists in the apparent nonexistence. Jesus said seek and ye shall find. Notice that first he said seek. Now if God wants us to find Him He will certainly make Himself known, and yet it has also been said that God loves our effort. We must put effort into this path, this journey which begins with an inquiry, who are we?

There is a reason this question keeps coming up, are we the elephant, the bear, the lion, who are we? Where do we find gratification, do we take it from the material world of earth, gold and sensual pleasure, do they satisfy us? Are they our reality or have we moved to a deeper center, a deeper world of meaning? Have we managed that difficult juggling act of pretending to believe in the world while actually believing in God? This means we look as if we have confidence in the structure of illusion, while at the same time recognizing we merely occupy its structure. Or have we taken confidence in illusion as the touchstone, the crown of our life? Which have we chosen? Do we think we are important because we have confidence in illusion, we have the titles this confidence in illusion confers? Have we sought the titles, do we chase after them or do we understand their limits, have we tried to control our relations with illusion?

We control our relations with illusion by domesticating the animal qualities, or else they run wild, they do not want to be in the background, they want to dominate. When a raccoon is cornered it can be vicious, difficult to deal with, and this is only on the outside, not on the inside where we fight the inner animals until we understand we cannot take the spiritual journey without the struggle. As we pass through the different worlds we begin to appreciate the rules or laws appropriate for different worlds, we learn the rules of domestication, a way to train our animal self. When a prophet was asked if he had no lower self he answered yes he had, but he had made it a believer, he had domesticated his animal qualities and made them work for human values.

We should understand this without reference to anyone but our own self, we should look at the struggle understanding who we are, who we are not, recognizing what we identify ourselves with, what we do not yet identify ourselves with, places within we have not so far discovered. Only when we begin to look closely can we understand because our dark side merely continues with a lack of introspection. Without it we are subject to each desire, to the different animal forms within us, each with a different agenda. We ride the current of desire if we fail to be introspective, if we fail to keep the animals under control, to domesticate them. When disturbed people are asked why they do bizarre things they often say they hear a voice in their head telling them what to do. If we wonder why they listen, we should be asking ourselves the same question, why do we listen, what are we thinking?

The mind is not our friend, it is a tool, not a friend. An axe can be used to cut down trees or to split someone's head, it depends on how it's used. The mind is not an axe, but it may control the arm which holds an axe. Consequence depends on our connection to what the mind tells us, those who are overrun by the mind can say and do bizarre things. There are those who have no problem with doing or saying whatever the mind dictates, and yet this is the opposite of an analysis which identifies right and wrong. We need a certain meter within saying right, wrong, right, wrong, when the meter registers wrong we say no. Without this meter there is no control, no system to assess what we do, and then we tend to identify ourselves with inappropriate things.

If we do the wrong thing long enough, we think that wrong thing is who we are; it becomes hard to create a new image for ourselves. We must create new images, if we are not changing we are dying, dying to reality, dying to truth. We are not the truth, we are on our way to truth, a way which requires the continuing ability to adapt ourselves to the aspect of truth shown to us, it requires the ability to leave everything behind we learned before which does not coincide with what we know now.

It is difficult for those who have a strong image of themselves to change, they have too much invested there. We should learn how to divest ourselves of that image, that pride, the self-importance, the elephant, the arrogance. Without doing this we cannot enter the path which has an opening too small for an elephant. If we think of ourselves as an elephant we will not get in, but an ant will, we have that little ant in us too. An ant works for its community, it has surrendered the self to a larger understanding. We should be part of a larger understanding.

The dualism of egocentric selfhood believes that anything given up is a loss, negative, something thrown away. As we give up arrogance, pride, ego, a sense of the differentiated self, something greater than anything we have known is available. As long as we cling to the differentiated self the greater thing is unavailable, that treasure is unavailable. The balancing act in the world, the straight, true path, is as fine as the edge of a sword. We are physical beings living in a physical world, we must maintain ourselves here, but also know who we are and obey the truth of who we are at the same time.

This path is about learning how to do this, actually doing it. There is a difference between knowing how and really doing it. We cannot accurately describe the taste of this as something that just happens to us, taste changes as we walk this path, we taste what we were never able to taste before. It comes with grace and it comes with effort, both ways. We should make the effort and open ourselves to grace. May we use these tools in a permissible way to bring us closer to Him, the one true treasure in existence.

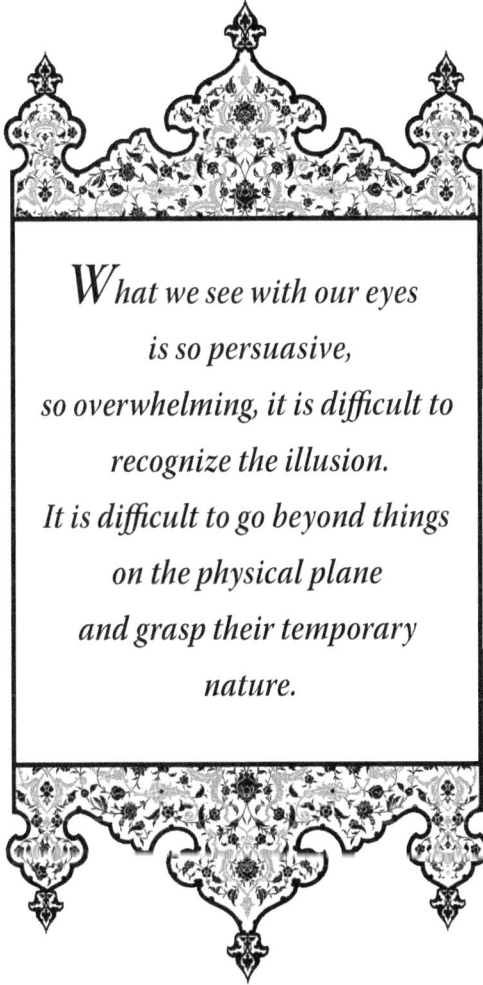

*What we see with our eyes
is so persuasive,
so overwhelming, it is difficult to
recognize the illusion.
It is difficult to go beyond things
on the physical plane
and grasp their temporary
nature.*

CHAPTER ELEVEN

The Drama of the World

What we see with our eyes is so persuasive, so overwhelming it is difficult to recognize the illusion. It is difficult to go beyond things on the physical plane and grasp their temporary nature. The physical plane is hypnotic, its effect is magnetic, it pulls us in inducing a condition which keeps us from seeing it for what it is. It sparkles, makes a noise, produces sound, it does things which affect us physically.

In a sense we have to protect ourselves from interacting with the physical world; if we are not prepared for what we encounter we are not ready to deal with it. When people grew their own food in earlier times they had to be ready for the physical reality of storms, heat, drought and rain, or they would not have had food to eat. This meant constant interaction with the world. How do we tell someone the grain they grow is illusion when they need this food to live, to survive?

The world gives us so many reasons to believe in its reality we are overcome just thinking about it, trapped and snared into thinking it is real. Also persuasive are the actions of other people we observe, they deal with the world as though it were real, their emotions are invested there. How do we deal with a world which is not real when people fight or struggle to get what they can from it, even though wise men insist it is not real? How do we develop the understanding that it is not real and yet we have to deal with it at the same time? This is the duality of existence, difficult to understand but a necessary understanding if we want to experience reality.

Most people cannot believe in what they do not see, cannot understand what they cannot grasp, and inevitably what they cannot understand does not exist for them. Some however, do have faith in things they do not understand, have faith in things they do not see because they realize their own limits. One problem which arises in the understanding of duality is recognizing our limits: only those who understand how much we do not know have some idea of all there is to know. For those who think they know, there is nothing left to learn, they are satisfied.

There is a small group who are not satisfied, who have an empty feeling after looking at all the things of the world. They still ask, "Who am I?" Now most people are more likely to ask, "Where am I going this evening?" "What am I having for dinner?" "What stock will make me money?" These are the questions in their consciousness they want answered, and they read daily newspapers to find the plays, concerts and exhibits to see, the current events to talk about with people who have nothing else to talk about. Although yesterday's newspaper is used to wrap the fish today, this is not part of most people's consciousness. Just because no one reads yesterday's newspaper does not stop us from reading today's, it does not stop us from commenting and talking about it, treating it as though it had importance. Here we have all the dramas of the world, all the dramas of our life, culturally, nationally and internationally.

Different people need different levels of drama; those who are pulled and pushed by their minds or their emotions think they are dead without the drama. When things are quiet, if they have only an outer life and no inner life, if there is nothing external to do they have no life, they have to make it up. How do they do that? With dramas like a soap opera on television going on day after day. We watch a soap opera for the unfinished drama inviting us to look again for the next installment.

We do the same thing in our own life as we are enmeshed in the unfinished dramas we do not end, do not care to play out or we will have to make up another one to take its place. Many marriages are dramatic and volatile, something can erupt at any moment to bring the drama to life. In the marriage drama we have someone to be angry with, someone to reconcile with, someone to stimulate all the emotions which make us feel alive. Those who bring peace to situations are rare, those who can dispense with the drama are rare. Few individuals understand that when the drama goes away, when the emotions go away, when the need for sensory stimulus goes away there is grace and a glory beyond anything else.

Most of us are so layered in our dramas, dramas in relationships, in emotions, there is no way we can penetrate all that, it is too dense, an avalanche we cannot dig out from, we need someone to bring in heavy machinery. Not many of us have the machinery for this avalanche, only a few. Most of us do not know we are buried in an avalanche because we are still breathing—we know we would have trouble breathing in an avalanche—only then do we know we are in trouble. As long as we are still breathing we do not recognize the trouble.

If we do not know we are in trouble, if we think there is a resolution to our drama, an end which will take us somewhere else, we are mistaken. Only with the experience of so many years looking at all the dramas will we realize there are no resolutions. The thrill is in the drama, the chase, the emotional roller coaster ends when we seemingly succeed. We get what we have strived for but do not know what to do with it, we have spent such a long time trying to get it, and now we do not know what to do with it. This kind of disappointment is sometimes called depression.

There is no cure for the drama or the obsessions of a world which offers no way out. It can only give us what it has, and all that it has is illusion. As long as we pay homage to the world and its illusions we are subject to it, ruled by it. The only way to escape is by giving homage to something else, making something else our priority, changing our focus, working on the inner transformation, finding contentment with something other than the world. We need to turn away from the world yet maintain our equilibrium there, turn away from the world yet work responsibly there.

We have to exist in two worlds simultaneously, only then is the paradox of our reality accounted for, only then is the truth available. The religions of the world are no different from any other illusion, they separate people, they say mine and yours, they say praise and blame, higher and lower. There is neither praise nor blame in reality, there is only truth, no mine and yours, there is only His in every circumstance. There are no differences between you and me in reality, no differences between my God and your God. God is One. When we create differences we are reacting as the world reacts, when we pull away from it we begin our repose in the truth.

There is a universal connection among us, we are made of the same things, we came from the same place, we return to the same place. We are only here for an interlude, a short time, which has become our reality. We need to learn the difference between this interlude and eternity, then treat the interlude appropriately. The notes of the interlude still have to be played correctly, but they are not the song, not all of it, they are merely part of it. Understand the part which is the world and the part which has no praise or blame. God is a beggar to a beggar and a king to a king. Whether we are beggars or kings the world is still an illusion, God is the same to us no matter our position, rank or status, they hardly matter if we are at peace, the peace which takes us to truth.

We must learn to focus correctly and stay in that focus, not letting ourselves be pushed and pulled, not letting the drama and mania of the world catch us. We have to be demagnetized, pass through a chamber altering our structure so that we are no longer magnetized, no longer hypnotized. This is the chamber of faith, certitude and determination, a chamber which knows that truth belongs to Him, obedience belongs to Him. To become who we truly are we surrender to that power controlling everything, a power both unseen and inexplicable. Believe we came from this power, we return to this power; everything exists in the right place, in the right way. May the peace of this understanding fill each heart, may our relationship with Him grow.

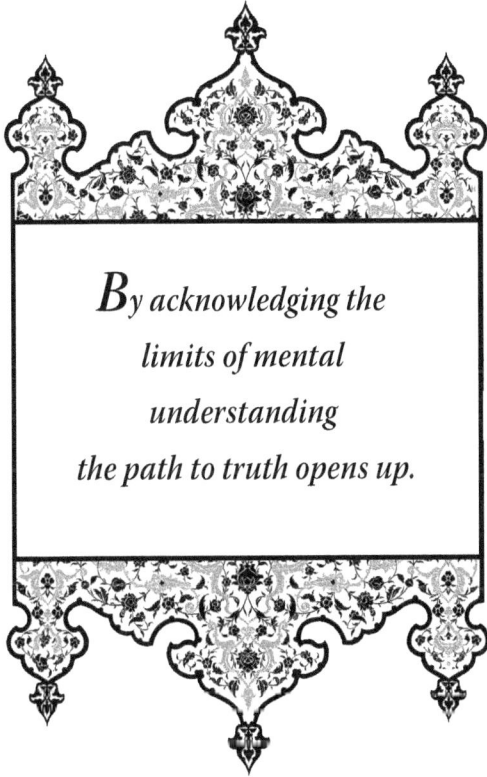

*By acknowledging the
limits of mental
understanding
the path to truth opens up.*

CHAPTER TWELVE

The Self and Reality

With the gift of sight we see what is in front of us, we are able to view the world. Now what we see is actually a reflection of light, but we perceive it as what lies in front of us. For most of us, the things we see with our eyes are what we call reality, some of us however, notice that what we see is not permanent, some of us realize that people disappear, things disappear.

This disappearance can make us wonder why. When we realize that people who were once here are no longer here, that friends we once had are no longer here, our parents are no longer here, we begin to contemplate certain things the world does not know how to explain. When it occurs to us that whatever happens to everyone else will eventually happen to us, we become students of the inexplicable, students of the mystery of existence. To understand what will happen to us we need to understand the nature of existence. We do see that we are all similar in some ways, we share characteristics and possibilities. Other things we do not see.

God created us, He created us as exalted beings, more exalted than the angels. In creating us He endowed us with certain faculties, the mind, intellect, the ability to be aware, to perceive things. We were created as a dependent thing, we are dependent on His creation and His sustenance, His maintenance of this world. When we open our eyes to look around we see His creation, each thing as dependent on Him as we are. We live our lives interacting with things which are dependent, things which are created, but these things are not part of the essential reality which is the Creator. What is real, what is dependent, what is our relationship to the dependent, what is our relationship to reality?

We have each been given an individuated consciousness, within the self we have the ability to think, to form words and use intellectual processes. Descartes, a French philosopher, concluded we can only prove our existence because we think, but enlightened teachers have told us when we engage the mind we are engaging illusion. In fact, we exist in a reality we cannot engage with if we are locked in the mind.

We have been given a separate mind, but the mind has been given limits. The secret is that as long as we fail to acknowledge its limited nature, we can never understand truth. By acknowledging the limits of mental understanding the path to truth opens up. What keeps us in illusion are the very thoughts making us think we are separate, different.

We have an attachment to this individuated being, this separate entity, to the illusion that it has independent existence. The mind is seductive because it can travel the world in the blink of an eye. If we close our eyes and think of the farthest place we have ever gone, how long does it take to get there? We are there in an instant, we can smell it, we can feel it and hear its sounds, that place exists inside our mind. Oceans exist there, the sky, the moon, the sun exist there and so do we. But these things are not actually substantial, they exist in a space inside our head like a vapor. Our life is like that, mere gas, like a thought, like thinking about existence, thinking about the places we have been, thinking about the things we have done, our history.

Just as all that thought has vanished everything else disappears too. Unless we understand the nature of this disappearance we can never escape from illusion; the insistence that the illusion is our existence keeps us from reality. We are dependent beings who are dependent on our Creator, on our Lord, yet we act as though we were independent.

Nevertheless, God has made our short-term, illusory existence important for that part of us which is permanent. The way we manage illusory existence determines whether we are capable of encountering reality; if our individuated being develops the ability to know that individuation is false, we can escape illusion and enter reality.

When we learn how to bypass the limits of the self we can discover our true nature. A key to bypassing them is to understand the nature of what exists now, acknowledging we are limited. If we are caught up in our individuated nature, if we make it so important that we never acknowledge its limits we cannot take the next step, we are satisfied with those limits, satisfied with the mind, the world, content to deal with creation as if it were reality.

We should recognize creation for what it is and know how it differs from reality. Even if we are unable to grasp that reality we need to know what is not real, we need to know what keeps us from moving towards it, know that our unlimited nature lies within the limited, individuated self. This is a great mystery. How can the key to reality exist within this limited nature?

We are attached to our limited nature, we dress it, we comb its hair, polish its nails, manicure its feet and do much more, we make it comfortable, we spend a lifetime taking care of it. At some point we need to cancel all that attention and say there is something more than this limited nature. If we are fortunate we encounter people who have had more experience along the path, far beyond our limited nature.

If we meet such people they tell us that life in this limited nature is essentially dualistic. People who live in that duality do not understand that all creation is one, that creation has come from one Creator. They do not understand that true knowledge exists. Nothing has to be discovered, all we have to do is let the truth be uncovered. It is not as if we were going to find something new.

Approaching reality means reducing the importance of the impermanent, the limited. The first steps become an ability to see our relation to reality, see the difference between our limited nature and reality. They are steps of recognition, we have some part of ourselves which wants to exist in reality. Yet we know we will disappear, our own experience tells us we will disappear, there are obituaries in the newspaper every day, on television we see people dying around the world. Everyone disappears from an elemental existence.

If we deny this, if we continue to live as if this were not happening, we might as well be consumed by the world because we are acting like a drunk even though we are sober. We are deluded, in a stupor, in confusion, we live in a fog that does not lift. We must lift the fog although the world refuses to let it lift, most of the world has no interest in lifting it, most of the religions are not interested in lifting it. The religions have changed, they came as a way to lift the fog, but they became institutions whose leaders were imperfect, who were preoccupied with their limited nature. They made themselves the religion and seized authority as though it were theirs.

Institutions all take us in the same direction. We need to go beyond them, while still learning the truth of each religion, because there is a truth buried there. The truth was given to this world by the prophets, men altered it, not God. The prophets brought the truth religions once had, a truth we have to go back to. We need to find people who teach, not for their own sake, for self-importance, not for power or wealth, but for the sake of the soul, being in touch with reality.

It has been said that we are to God as the pupil is to the eye. Think about the eye, the pupil is the opening which lets in light allowing us to see, it permits vision by its nonexistence, it does not get in the way. God created us so that He would be able to see Himself, we are the pupil of His eye. We know if the pupil of our eye is blocked the world has altered focus, if we use a colored lens we see different colors, if we put veils before our eyes we see things differently, our vision is altered. The pupil must be pure, clear and without obstruction, human beings must be pure, clear and without obstruction.

What is the veil between ourselves and reality? Our belief in ourselves, we are what separates us from reality; when we understand the nature of that separation, when we understand we are clinging to illusion and let it go, the veils are lifted, the pupil is open, no obstruction, God can see God. Until that happens all we see is the creation, not even that, the illusion of creation, the images we create in our mind, the images we create with our mind as we open and close our eyes. The mind loves to enlarge what we see, to take a picture and enlarge it. The mind does create alternatives, if we do not like the picture we shut the world down and dream while we are awake.

We need to understand this individuated being holds the key to our eternal existence. If our individuated self does not act correctly our chance to engage eternal existence is lost, but if we act correctly, if we make that individuated self disappear our opportunity is open, we can move from duality. This opportunity is in our own hands, it lies within the given, in the hands of our perspective, our attitude.

We change our attitude by saying even though I cannot understand certain things, cannot understand what is all around me, my experience leads me to believe I cannot trust the created, it leads me to conclude if I depend on the things of the world I will be disappointed. There must be something else.

Then we begin the search for that something else. Jesus said seek and ye shall find. We have to put great effort into this search with discipline, with faith in what we cannot understand. We need both principles and practices.

Many of us were born into certain beliefs, into a religion. If we have not been guided to the truth we should think now, "What I have been taught so far directs me to the world, not to God. I need to find my way there." We need to find someone who guides us and satisfies our hunger to know the truth. May we all discover this path of truth.

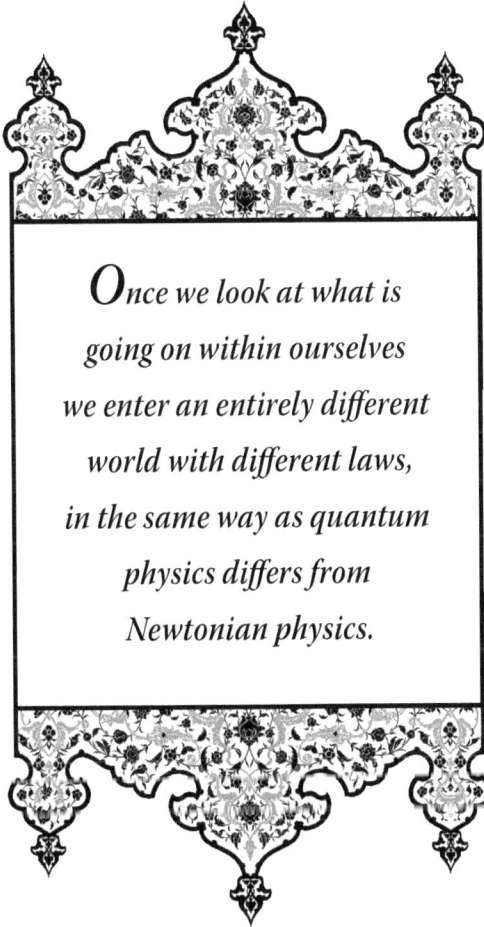

Once we look at what is
going on within ourselves
we enter an entirely different
world with different laws,
in the same way as quantum
physics differs from
Newtonian physics.

Elemental Disturbances

The circumstances of our daily lives often overwhelm us, make us want to shout, "Stop!" We want all that momentum to stop, we want something at rest, something at peace. What we do to find that rest and peace depends on the things we have learned, it depends on an understanding of existence, the nature of reality. Some of us think if we change those worldly circumstances we will find a peaceful place, we will alter the space where we exist. By changing our environment, by changing our surroundings, we will change how we feel.

We might have learned that changing our environment just changes our environment, it does not have much to do with our relationship to the world, it takes something else to alter the way we relate to things. This change comes some other way which does not have much to do with what is going on around us, it has more to do with what is going on inside. Once we look at what is going on within ourselves we enter an entirely different world with different laws, in the same way as quantum physics differs from Newtonian physics. Newtonian physics describes the world we see, but it cannot account for the subatomic world. Quantum physics tries to explain how minute, invisible particles move and work, something quite different from the physics of visible, larger things.

In the same way, things which help us find success in the world do not necessarily help us find inner peace, worldly success does not help us find inner peace. Watch an elephant solving problems, notice it does this by running over things, stamping them out, getting them out of its way. Some people and some countries think this is a way to solve problems. People and animals tend to deal with problems by moving things around, altering things by force. This might make us think that to get things done we have to use force, action. The rules for inner peace are exactly opposite, we do not force things, we learn to disengage. Think how different these two words are, force and disengage.

Consider the anxiety which is caused by fear, a problem for so many. Fear is there for different reasons, but most often it is worry about the future, believing we might lose something, imagining harm. If we can eliminate anticipation of the future, projecting situations which might occur, and live in each moment as it is, things do change, with difficulty, but they do change. The difficulty comes from living in the mind which is incapable of conceiving right now. The mind's natural habitat, its only habitat, is the future or the past, it fluctuates between them. Studies have found that memory exerts as strong an influence as the events of the moment, its control is just as powerful. Our mind cannot recognize the difference between the past, the future, and what is happening right now, it cannot tell the difference. We are tied to whatever our mind wanders through until we know that thoughts of the future and the past are as powerful as the present moment, then we can work to disengage that stream of ideas pushing us this way and that. To find peace we have to stop all the action we are subjected to by the mind.

The waves in the ocean never stop, they are pulled by gravitational forces, by the moon. We are pulled by the same forces, we are composed physically of the same elemental forces which surround us, but until we realize they are not who we are, every time there is an elemental reaction we feel pulled. Think of anger as a tornado, think of a violent outburst as a thunderstorm inside, natural, elemental things that happen. If we were outdoors in a thunderstorm we would try to find shelter, we would go inside. If we are the thunderstorm, do we realize we are inflicting thunder, lightning and rain on everyone we come near, do we realize that this is just an elemental eruption? Do we recognize that we can be volcanoes? What good does it do to know these things? It does good only if our consciousness can be detached from these things to watch. If there is a thunderstorm while we sit inside looking out the window we can be calm about it. If there is a tornado approaching and we are protected, the damage can be minimal, but if we try to run from it the damage might be catastrophic.

How do we detach ourselves from things which upset us, how do we detach the uproar of our life? We begin by choosing new priorities. The world selects its priorities quite simply, it counts what it has and what it does not have, just as our lower self chooses. The animals within us all want something, they function according to what they get or fail to get. As long as we accept our animal priorities we are part of the food chain, we are out there eating or trying not to be eaten. If we withdraw from that, if we can stop the world's effect on us by refusing that interaction, we can change, we can learn the laws of inner life, the laws of reality.

We begin to understand these laws when we no longer have likes and dislikes, when we are no longer dependent on praise and blame. In the world of praise and blame we like people because they praise us, we dislike people because they blame us, we like people who give us things, we do not like people who do not give us things. Children like people who give them toys, if we give them enough they run up to us with pleasure, if we stop they think we have changed, we used to be nice, not now. We should see this in ourselves, realize that these childish behavior patterns have not changed very much.

Our expectations have to change, we should understand the journey of this life in a new way, actually believe it. Easy enough to say the appropriate things, different to live it. Are we happy for the success of others, are we joyous because others are joyous, sad because they are sad, hungry when they are hungry? What does it take to satisfy us? Can we offer all our praise to God whether our glass is full, half full or one quarter full? There is a traditional story that when the prophet Muhammad and his companions were going through difficult times, they were truly satisfied with less. The operative word here is satisfied, an important aspect in our state of being is satisfaction.

What does it take to satisfy us, to be at peace, do we need some outer affirmation, have we conditioned ourselves to require external specifics? Have we learned instead to be satisfied that God is merciful, that He protects us? Have we learned we are His creation, He exists within us, we can be in contact with Him? If this is the touchstone of our existence life changes, the way we see things changes, yet as we rush through the world we can lose touch with this understanding. All those worldly influences have an impact on us, the hypnotic effect of the world has an impact on us, the whole world pulls us. Our state of being is affected unless we take certain countermeasures, find periods of time when we deliberately disconnect from the world, when we say stop, this is a moment to disconnect.

We have to tell ourselves the world is not real and live some part of our life believing that, believing we do not need it, we are not dependent on it. If we live as though we are dependent on the world we believe our sustenance comes from there. If we believe our sustenance comes from the world, that this is what keeps us going, when we come to the end of everything there is a great vacuum, a failure to understand. We should know that our inner life is different from every aspect of outer life, something else is going on here. The laws of this inner life are different from the laws of the world. The saints give us examples of lives which have adjusted to inner and outer, they are more concerned about others than about themselves, they are ready to help without being asked, ready to give themselves, withholding nothing. They have lost any motive of self, they have only God's motive, accepting the equality of all beings, equating others with themselves. Once when just such a saint finished telling someone in great detail about that person's failings, he concluded by saying, "But that does not make me any better than you."

This is important, if we think becoming holy makes us better than others we have lost the understanding of what we are doing. We have merely substituted pride for physical possessions. In the formless world there are formless things we can be attached to which have the same bad effect that things in form have. Detaching ourselves from the world of forms is not the solution. Things that exist as form also have a formless counterpart. Wanting to amassing large amounts of money has a formless state called greed, wanting to acquire the ability to control others has a formless state called power. We should be aware of the inappropriate formless states we must also detach ourselves from, know there is an essence within each form we can be in touch with instead. To go there takes concentration, it takes effort and work.

Can we pull ourselves from anxiety, move away from inappropriate feelings and concentrate on truth, can we loose the hold of illusion and every false thing? Reading scriptures, reading the holy books centers us in a way which helps us take these steps. We must be centered or we cannot do it. We cannot be wondering how something will turn out and concentrate on God at the same time, we cannot be wondering about a woman or a man and concentrate on God at the same time, we cannot be thinking about personal relationships, how others have hurt us and concentrate on God at the same time. We have to leave all this behind.

How much internal baggage do we have, how much of our history do we keep revisiting with every step we take? How do we put all these burdens down, relieve ourselves of these things? First we become aware of them, become aware of what they do, then we can let them go. This is not something we have to do just once, this is something we have to do again and again. It has taken a lifetime to collect these hidden things, to clean them out takes a great effort, but it can be done. When we wash for prayer we must also wash inwardly, be cleansed of hypocrisy, be cleansed of every fault. We must not divide our life into segments where we allow what we should always disallow. We should not give space to what we think is not who we are, we should not fragment experience but live as an integrated being who dominates our consciousness all the time, whose voice we know so well we automatically exclude the sounds of any lower consciousness. We are lost without that integrated being who keeps us from doing what we are not supposed to do.

All our enemies live inside us, not outside. We must identify the inner enemies which are more treacherous than anything on the outside. We sabotage ourselves with the things the animal part of us likes and wants, we sabotage ourselves with large and small desires. As long as we take pleasure in anything but God our life is fragmented, we allow parts of us to do whatever they like. This path expects us to model ourselves on the lives of saints, it expects us to become a friend of God, like the saints. This is not a special place, it is an appropriate place, one which is cleansed, not better, just a place, reality not unreality.

We have a decision to make, do we want to live in illusion or in reality, a decision we make every day, every moment, with every interaction in our life. This awareness makes us more deliberately conscious of what we do. Once we understand and accept it we should not waver, once we choose it we should not take it up and put it down when it suits us. This is not an easy path, we must keep making the decision. It is a struggle, we do have to keep fighting, that is the reason it is called a struggle. God understands how difficult it is for us, all we have to do is what we have to do, keep moving forward. Let us not be upset by a difficult state, God is on our side, He wants us to understand the truth. Merging with the truth does not mean losing anything, it means becoming part of everything. What we actually lose is anxiety, the anxiety of individuation, the fears and difficulties of individuation. We become part of a glorious cornucopia, gifts without end, mercy without end. When we give up things we mistakenly took to be positive, something much greater becomes available.

What we look at outwardly is illusory, it will pass and disappear, it is not real. Understand the temporary nature of this existence, we are here to understand the permanent, not the temporary. God holds the key to the gate of the permanent. May that key be used to allow us entrance into God's permanent reality.

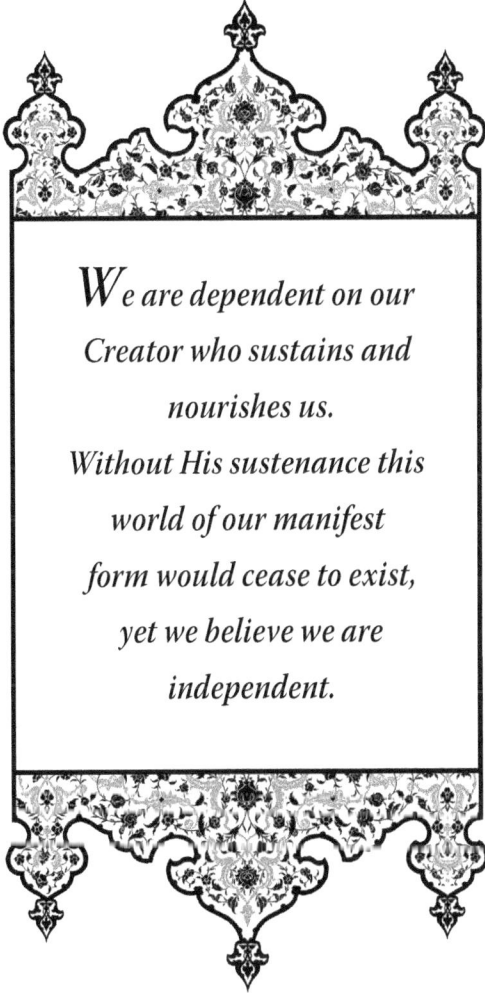

*We are dependent on our
Creator who sustains and
nourishes us.
Without His sustenance this
world of our manifest
form would cease to exist,
yet we believe we are
independent.*

CHAPTER FOURTEEN

Dependent and Independent

An embryo is connected by the umbilical cord to its mother, a feeding tube which delivers nourishment. After the baby's birth the cord is cut and this direct attachment is discontinued, but the baby still takes sustenance from the mother through its mouth. The baby has not yet developed all the levels of consciousness which an adult has, although this limited consciousness understands where its sustenance comes from, it knows that it needs to be near its mother.

When children are young, at one, two or three years old they do not like being away from their mother. Since she has been their source of food and comfort, separation from that source can be frightening. By the age of four they usually lose this persistent attachment to their mother, they wander a little, they eat more independently. For some this dependence on the mother lasts longer, for some less, but that parent who was once the source of everything for the child becomes gradually less relevant in its life.

Different things happen to the individual as this dependence is lost, they forget the dependence on the mother and father they once had. Sometimes they think these parents they used to cling to have not much to offer, have little to tell them, and they find other sources of information. Sometimes the children are right and sometimes they are wrong.

Just as we forget we were a totally dependent being in our

embryonic stage, and we forget we were still dependent as a small child, if our arrogance builds we lose sight of that dependent state entirely. We do not realize that even though we are no longer connected by an umbilical cord or to a mother's breast, we are still dependent. A great lie of the world is that as we mature, as we grow up, we become independent; we do not.

We are dependent on our Creator who sustains and nourishes us. Without His sustenance this world of our manifest form would cease to exist, yet we believe we are independent. There are many ways to explain why people feel independent, but it matters only that all these explanations are false. As we go through life we believe we are doing things on our own, we forget how everything has been set in place for us, how everything has been established for us. Once we lose our gratitude for this we feel a sense of independence, we think we are a separate individual because we are not connected in a way we can see. If we are connected we think we are dependent, we are like a television set, plugged in it works, otherwise it does not. We deduce we must have our own battery pack making us independent. Since this is untrue, we have to separate ourselves from this misconception to learn the truth about ourselves.

The world tries to glorify our independence, tells us how great we are, gives us dinners and awards, immortalizes us in different halls of fame. Our language deceives us, using words to alter a reality which cannot be changed. The truth is we are dependent, as dependent as an embryo attached to the umbilical cord, as dependent as a baby at its mother's breast.

Since the dependence we have is not so obvious, so evident, we need to develop levels of subtlety which let us see things not obvious or evident. The world deals with the obvious, newspapers and television tell us what is going on at superficial levels, on the surface, they do not delve beneath the surface, they write for an immature audience, the lowest common denominator. We should look within and understand our dependence as we did when we were babies and feared separation from our parents, we were lost without them. We should fear separation from our Lord because we are lost without Him, we should be conscious that either we have a connection to our Lord or we have lost it. Our connection is not outer, it is inner. Do we have that consciousness of God, are we conscious of what He does, that He sustains and nourishes us, that He cares for us, or have we lost this consciousness? If we have lost our God-consciousness we have lost the capacity to be raised above an animal state.

Although we are not connected outwardly, physically, we are connected in reality where there is no physical attachment. What is physical is not reality. We have a light body within us which is our reality, a connection we must be conscious of. This connection to God which lives within us exists on a level of consciousness, a level deep within the heart we need to be aware of. To be aware of it we have to engage specific qualities, qualities like gratitude. Gratitude is a door opening our connection to God, it permits an understanding of Him we cannot have without it. We are grateful to those who help us, and who helps us more than our Lord? What do we do when we are grateful to someone? We try to help them, be of use to them, but what could God want from us? He wants us to live with His qualities, to experience mercy, to experience compassion and all His qualities, He wants us to be as much like Him as we can. Once we understand this relationship with our Father, once we enter through that door of gratitude, become obedient because we are so overwhelmed by what He has done for us, then we can start to be a true human being, we can build a life integrated with His qualities.

The words integrated and integrity are close to each other. Integrity implies a depth in our qualities which is not false, it is genuine. We do not merely talk about these things, we know this state of being, we have become this state of being. Mercy is our touchstone, compassion, compliance with His justice, this is our touchstone. Love for others is the key to our interaction with them because love is the key to His interaction with us. Everything comes from that love, His love for us. The totality of the universe He created lies within each of us, put there so that we could experience Him, and He could experience us. His residence is love, His action is love, His countenance is love, His vibration is love, His name is love.

We need to be the bearers of this love. Everything preventing its existence must be removed, things like the arrogance of selfhood, the arrogance of believing we are better, separate, somehow above, more distinguished, more important because we wear more medals, we have more dinners to honor us, we have more degrees. We need to be rid of each self-centered motivation which rises up as we put the self on a pedestal. Without this egocentric impulse other things become possible. The world tells us that becoming the same reduces us, if we lose our individual self we are less, but with the loss of all this individuation His glory is available, knowledge of Him is available, and the door to reality opens. The veil separating us from reality is a refusal to give up selfhood, individuation, yet once we do there is a light beyond our ability to describe, to imagine or think about.

This light exceeds the capacity of our intellect, its splendor hypnotizes the mind which is now truly afraid, it knows it will disappear once that light is acknowledged. Since this is not what the mind wants we have to talk to it, convince it there is nothing to be afraid of, whatever happens will be good for us. Then we can end the struggle, the conflict between the process of individuation and the process of disappearing, the conflict between becoming bigger and becoming smaller. It will stop, although it takes a certain determination, a certain ability to convince the mind to leave us alone. If we do not accept this struggle the mind will run away with us, we have to tame the shrew living inside us. This shrew, this lower self must be tamed, it is not going away, it will always be there, but it must be under our control.

The prophet Muhammad was once asked if he had a lower self, if he had base desires. He answered that he had, but his desires had become believers. This is what we have to do, make our desires believers, then we can all be servants of the Lord. If we watch ourselves through the day we will observe all the inclinations we have, the inclinations of the universe existing within us. Each aspect of this world within us, except for that light put there by God's breath, has an inappropriate inclination. We should watch our inclinations and determine which are appropriate and which are not—just because an inclination presents itself does not mean we have to accept it. This is a simple kind of analysis, but it does entail constant vigilance. If we are not aware of our inclinations, unaware of where and how they originate, we are led astray. Making a correct assessment is what we have to do. May God help us with this struggle.

*It is important to realize
how much we can be prisoners
of our thoughts,
jailed in a space inside
our own head.*

Escape From the Mind

It is important to realize how much we can be prisoners of our thoughts, jailed in a space inside our own head. Unless we know this we might be walking around believing we are free, when, in fact, we cannot make a move without the implicit approval of our mind. This is a problem for ourselves and for the world. Certain individuals who are the most confined and controlled by their minds are also persuaded they are right, they know best, they have been appointed to spread what they know. The more our mind controls us, the more we try to control all those around us.

Whatever goes on inwardly is what we present outwardly, another good reason to pay attention to what goes on within, to avoid reacting on automatic. Philosophies have been founded on concepts of the world as a place with no exit. We need a different way of thinking, a way of looking at creation which shows us that light is available, we do not have to see everything as closed up tight, impenetrable. We ourselves are closed up if we think we know the answer, if we think we know what is going to happen because we alone have a complete idea of what is going on. What we need is a state of mind which includes the possibility that we do not know, the expectation, even the certainty, that there is knowledge beyond us. The humility of this certainty, this way of thinking, is a key to the open space of freedom.

If we do not have the humility to recognize there is something greater than we are, something which knows more than we do, that there is something we can learn from our companions or from the rest of humanity, if we do not have that openness we are locked away from reality. We need the understanding which teaches us to treat other people appropriately; not only is it good for others when we are kind, but it is also what can save us. Without kindness we ruin ourselves and make life difficult for everyone else. They will ignore us if they are wise, but if we influence them they end up like us.

We need to understand just how we communicate with our own self, how we listen to ourselves, how we react to ourselves. Without this understanding we have not started the journey, without self-examination there is no path, anything we realize occurs accidentally. When we make a commitment to the path we begin with self-examination, here in the place where we encounter our first difficulties, because now we see our negative side, we see the pain it has caused. If we cannot face the remorse this causes, if we do not have the courage to face that pain we stop looking, we turn away, not believing what we see is true. We go back to jail, we stop trying to find a way out and cancel the ability to escape.

To escape there must be effort, without effort the only way to escape is with a revolution that opens the jails, what the religions teach. They say a messiah will save us, a messiah will save us all. Jailbreak. What are the chances this revolution will happen in our lifetime, how long have we been told the jailbreak is coming, how many have said the jailbreak has already happened? The religions have been promising a messiah for thousands of years, yet how many millions and millions have already died, how long are we supposed to sit and wait? Our responsibility is to be our own messiah, something we can aspire to if our way of thinking and our thoughts focus on becoming a perfected human being. If the way we see the world includes the path to enlightenment, if there is the faith, certitude and determination that this can happen there is liberation for us. Of course, some will tell us we are mistaken, while others will say it can happen for them but not for us. When they fail to see the possibility of enlightenment in others they have blocked their own possibility, if we cannot see it in others there is no possibility for ourselves. This is a key to understanding, seeing the possibility in others. When we hear people speaking in a way which denigrates others, which treats others as diminished, less than they are, we should walk away from the conversation, they cannot help anyone. If we stop to listen we are encouraging something that will not continue without an audience, if we stop to listen that way of thinking might impose itself, enclose us in the jail of the mind. This is a disease we must avoid.

In life we encounter many perspectives, many useless points of view which take us away from the truth. People who feel compelled to be in control usually take charge, they probably have the driving obsession it takes to be a leader, are willing to make the great effort to stay ahead of those biting at their heels. We frequently end up with leaders for whom control is an obsession. We rarely find people leading groups with something other than a closed mind, an obsession promising power, their escape from the dominance of others. But it is only the mind telling them power will give them what they want, what they need. This is one of the great lies of the world, and yet such people have become leaders of religions and nations, imposing their obsessive perspective on the culture of a country. Once this is established in the culture, children are born to it, they accept what they are told from infancy because they hear the lie again and again until they are no longer critical, they just believe it. We have so many gods, the first is our mother, the second our father, the third is our teacher at school. If all these gods tell us the same thing our chance to escape their methods is slim, and yet that possibility does exist, that opportunity comes to each of us at some time, at some critical juncture of our existence.

When we catch a glimpse of something extraordinary, something like love, this can change everything. When we experience love things like pride, nationality, jealousy, all suddenly have less meaning. Once we recognize the frailty of the human condition, pride of religion and race disappear; once we recognize the sameness in every human being everything else disappears; in such moments we can escape, the lie is lit up, we can run away.

Scriptures speak of the difficulties the prophets had telling their people the truth. They did not need what a prophet said, what their parents told them was enough. The world is not open to new ideas, but God in His mercy has sent messengers to shatter a stubborn state of mind, the closed jail cell of the mind, to shatter the culture which binds and ties us. If we listen, if we begin to examine ourselves we can break out of that cell. The work begins with self-examination, with an understanding that the way the mind speaks to us, the things it engages are not the way out, the way lies beyond the capacity of the mind.

Movies are nothing more than pictures on a screen, they are shadows, colored shadows. The mind cannot differentiate interaction with human beings from interaction with colored shadows, it takes its emotion from a television screen, from a colored shadow we react to as if the events projected actually had occurred. Then we describe what we saw as an extraordinary emotional experience, it moved us to the roots of our being. When was the last time we were moved to the roots of our being because we saw a certain quality in a person, we saw the possibility of truth in him? When was the last time we were moved to the roots of our being because we saw that possibility in ourselves, the time when we recognized what was available and felt depths of sorrow for not accepting what we might have become? We should focus on that possibility and pray for it. With humility, understanding how little we are, we should beg God to allow us that possibility. He has sent so many wise, holy beings to tell us this is His intention, He has sent so many prophets to tell us this is His intention for us. Should we not align ourselves with God's intention, should we fight against it?

The world tells us wait, it will happen in the future, someone will come to save us, yet we long for instant enlightenment. God loves our effort, but we say give me a pill, make me enlightened now. God loves our effort, we are His mystery and He is our mystery. How are we involved in this play of ours, do we merely behave like the ingénue who says and does nothing, merely reacting to others, or are we engaged? Is our focus strong or are we pulled about by everything all around us? We can push ourselves in the right direction, we know where to get help, we can be recentered, refocused, we can understand and have a vision of truth. We do have something appropriate in our own memory, we do have moments when we glimpsed reality. We should use the memory of such special moments as a springboard to leave the mind and go to the heart, use that to bring us into the reality of this moment.

If we need inspiration we already have it, something different for each of us, but we do have it. We can use that memory to project us from the mind, to escape from it. Memory can recall the experience of not being in the mind, use this aspect of mind as a tool to release us from the mind. This mind is not our master, it is a tool we can use appropriately to take us where we are supposed to go, otherwise it will make us a slave. Open the door to the jail and throw away the key, we are free.

Lies which are repeated again and again, no matter how false, are eventually believed. A lie detector will not pick up a lie if we believe what we are saying. For the most part we do not remember accurately, our mind often twists what has happened to make it favorable to ourselves, and this is what we remember. Even when we think our memory is favorable in a more general way, we are not always right. We should be aware of our mind, the dangers of the mind, we should be aware of our culture, the dangers of culture. We need to know how we think and what has made us think the way we do. Our freedom lies in escape from patterns of thought which have locked us in jail. Escape from the mind to the heart, our freedom lies through the heart. May that path be open to us all.

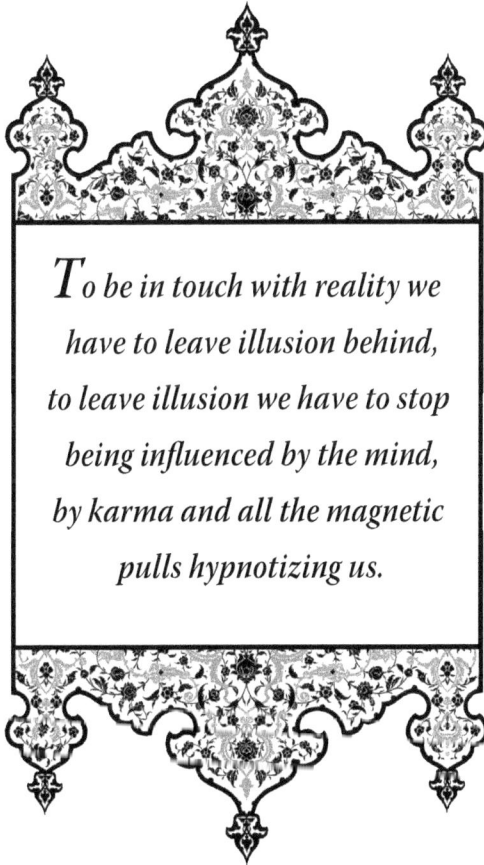

CHAPTER SIXTEEN

*To be in touch with reality we
have to leave illusion behind,
to leave illusion we have to stop
being influenced by the mind,
by karma and all the magnetic
pulls hypnotizing us.*

Karma

Understanding what it means to say we are taking something too personally gives us a key to understanding truth. People are offended when they feel they have been forced into a position they neither want nor deserve. The driver of a car will chase another driver because he has been cut off, behaving as though it were a deliberate, personal affront although they have never met before. What does it mean when we take this sort of thing personally, what does it mean to be offended, to go beyond acceptable boundaries? What does it mean when our pride, our consciousness of self interferes with an ability to act, what is the origin of such feelings? Why are some people so distraught they shout and carry on about a minor situation? All this comes from an exaggerated sense of self, the bigger that sense of self the more we protect it, the more space it needs, the more it bumps into, making life more difficult. Some people think of themselves as imposing and tall even if they are small and short. This is an exaggerated sense of self, exaggerated pride in their own importance.

What conclusions can we take from this exaggerated sense of self? We see that the more attached we are to the things of the world, the more important they are to us, the greater our sense of self. If titles, position and fame are important to us we react violently to anything which affects title, position or fame, we have made them our priorities. If they are less important our reactions are different. For some people reactions are attached to an emotional center which is out of control, it is so much a part of who they are reactions occur spontaneously, without any thought process, almost instinctively. When someone says something a certain way there is a reaction, an immediate reaction we call temper, a predisposition which triggers great difficulty.

What is this predisposition, what makes us react this way? Now we have to talk about karma, what it is, and a way to understand it. Karma is our attachment to the world and all the reactions connected to that attachment, karma is interlaced with a personal sense of self which keeps us here, which blocks a more transcendent state. When we have empathy for others we break through that sense of self as our attention is focused in a different way, in a different place. Breaking our attention on the self shuts down both our karma and our attention to the world. We need to reduce any inflated sense of self, not just mentally or in what we say, we have to incorporate this in our actions, be more subtle, become a person who actually thinks about what we are doing. If we can do this it will shut down our karmic reaction longing to erupt.

A famous Greek orator who understood the power of speech, the power of the tongue, kept pebbles in his mouth to prevent himself from speaking before he could think. We need to do something like that, not just applied to our tongue, but to our mental processes, to all the instinctive karmic reactions which seem to pop out of us. Karma is not only something we acquire as we go through our life, it is also something we inherit, like the color of our hair. We have to know what we are born with and work on it, learn how to do the work, then we can begin to change. When we reduce our karma we reduce our sense of self, we are closer to something beyond the self as we set out on the path to truth, to reality otherwise what we are doing is merely make-believe. If we are self-indulgent and hallucinatory we can produce any scenario to keep us entangled in all these karmic influences.

We are not going to find reality by thinking things through, even though thinking can be a useful tool when our mind is not lying to us. Because the mind is a great liar we need to identify an observer which does not come from the mind. Scott Peck is a Christian psychologist who wrote The People of a Lie some years ago, an interesting book about people he had diagnosed who kept lying to him. They came for help, but they did not actually want to be helped, and there was nothing he could do. He understood all these people had one thing in common, they lied. He recognized they had something going on which breached the bounds of normality, something had caught them, like a demon. Their minds were so strong they were being lead around, but every once in awhile they would catch a glimpse of their situation and go for help. Eventually, he found the only way to help these people was with exorcism. We all have dark forces trying to attack us, the great liar working through the mind.

How do we escape, how do we get away from all this? We do this by creating a space in ourselves where the world has no meaning, where everything we have held dear disappears. We need time in our life to focus this way, to focus as if we were no longer here. Imagine ourselves already gone—what was the use of everything we once clung to, pride, self-interest, personality, delusions, what happens when all that is gone? This is what early morning meditation is about, this is the place where we have an opportunity to release our karma, an opportunity to be rid of that binding, earthly attachment which is less powerful early in the morning. When these hypnotizing, magnetic pulls are weaker we have the opportunity to see clearly, to break some of the chains binding us to the world. This is the purpose of meditation, the focus of meditation. We break our normal thought patterns, remove the things which push, pull and guide us, more or less instinctually now because we have been like that for so long.

The routines of our daily life have habituated us to status, to our place in the order of things. We have created an inner caste system which gives the self a place everything is consolidated around. No one created this for us, we did it by ourselves to ourselves, a position we have created and try desperately to maintain. This is the karma we have to break free of, break through, we have to break these chains we bound ourselves with, the delusions we created, the thoughts, images and hallucinations we created to define our world. We need to let the world be defined by the way it is, by reality, not ourselves.

The only way to do this is to be in touch with reality. To be in touch with reality we have to leave illusion behind, to leave illusion we have to stop being influenced by the mind, by karma and all the magnetic pulls hypnotizing us. We need to spend time in a clear place praying to God saying we understand, we understand the confusion we live with, the illusions we swim in. We need to say we have no interest in that anymore, take it away from us, this is not ours, we just thought it was all these years. We say God take this away because as soon as we begin to think about ourselves we are back in the same trap. You must do it, how can we possibly do this? Make us see the truth, take us from this illusion we have made our life, offer us the fragrance of reality.

This is the way things change when we come upon truth, we are not bound by the things of the world, everything changes. We have to believe this can happen even if we have not seen it before, that does not mean it will not happen. If we have not seen it we have not wanted to see it urgently enough. Someone once asked a wise teacher how he could know if he wanted God enough. They happened to be standing beside a lake, the teacher put the student's head in the water, holding him there. When he pulled him out he said, "When you want God as much as you wanted your next breath, you want God enough."

That is the point, we have to be so tired of the way we have lived we make space in our life to be free, even if only for an hour each day. We need accumulating practice in the realm of truth. We need to keep doing this because we are not good at remembering, we fall back into old habits. We need to create appropriate new habits. The tools which once took us the wrong way can take us the right way if we break bad habits and create good habits, if we throw away old desires and create new desires, if we yearn for the right things. This is the only choice we have to make, we choose the world or we choose God, and we cannot be deceived. We have to look at every choice we make to see where it takes us, we have to do this every day, all the time.

We need to break the hold the world has on us and enter reality. This is the straight path. May God be our guide on this path and show us the way.

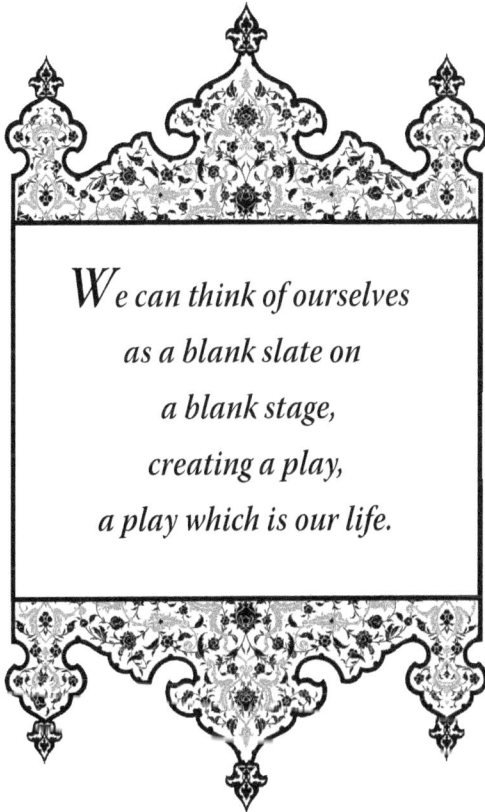

*We can think of ourselves
as a blank slate on
a blank stage,
creating a play,
a play which is our life.*

Actor and Audience

Shakespeare famously proclaimed all the world is a stage and the men and women merely players. An interesting idea, being an actor in this world, yet if we are actors we are also the audience, we participate as both actors and audience. As actors, to whom do we play, as audience, to whom do we listen? Answers to these two questions can tell us something about ourselves, tell us about attitude, about what we consider important, what we try to accomplish, where we are going in this world.

As a child we play to our parents, different emotions for different needs to get what we want. When we develop language we continue playing to our parents, only now we use words instead of cries and yells. At the same time we are also the audience for our parents, they play to us, imprinting their play on us. Especially when we are so young, the acts they play have a deep influence on us, on the act we will develop, the first draft of the script for our life. We are told that what is written on us when we are young is carved in stone, what is written later when we are older is written on water. What is etched in stone when we are young stays with us a long time. It is difficult to change these deep grooves, to maneuver our way out requires a great effort.

At the beginning of life we are given a script by our parents before we are able to determine whether it is good, mediocre or bad, so much of the script is just imprinted. As actors we need a script, but where does it come from, what is the reason for it, what is behind it? A play or a movie usually targets an audience, the script is developed for a certain audience. Who is our target, what script are we using to target this audience, who is it we want watching us, who is it we need to have watching us? Do we interact with whoever is watching? Then in the audience part of our life, who is it we watch, why do we watch, why do we interact with it?

There is a story about a sheikh who told all his disciples to kill a chicken when no one was looking. A few hours later they had all come back except for one slow disciple. When they laughed asking him why he had not killed his chicken, he just stood there shaking. Then the sheikh asked them to tell what they did, and each one told his story, where they killed their chicken, where no one saw them. Finally, the slow disciple said, "There was nowhere God was not watching." This is an old teaching story with an important point, who is our audience, who is it we have made our audience, are we aware of our audience, do we know that God is watching?

If we know that God is watching, what have we done to make the script appropriate for this audience, to fill our life with things this audience appreciates, to make our act appropriate for this audience? Are we still acting for an audience which confers praise, which fulfills desires or grants worldly acceptance, wealth, anything we think we can get from the world? If we decide that God is our audience we have to develop the script for an appropriate act. As an actor, the action of our life must be suitable for God's presence, appropriate for God as our audience. Whether we accept this or not, He is our audience.

In our worldly audience who is the critic assessing the play? Different critics have different criteria, if our audience is an audience of thieves they will judge our ability to steal, if it is an audience of murderers they will judge our ability to murder, if it is a military audience they will judge our ability to fight, if our audience is professional they will judge our ability in our profession. We create the audience and we create the act, we are responsible for both the audience and the act. Once we decide the world is no longer our audience, that God is our audience, where do we find the right script, what do we need to learn? When we think about this we remember that scriptures explain how to act appropriately for God, but they are open to interpretation, so much interpretation. We need to assess what is appropriate, something never easy or straightforward. We choose, we make the decisions which determine our own actions, our development or loss.

We ourselves are the root cause which determines where we go, that root cause is our responsibility, we determine what the intention should be. As we choose our course we select the audience which determines the act we play, how we see ourselves determines the person who plays our act. Do we see ourselves as God's greatest creation, as He describes us, or do we see ourselves as unworthy, incapacitated? On the other hand, do we see ourselves as someone who needs no help, someone who can do everything on his own, someone who has great power, the power to move the world? We ignore God for different reasons. How do we see ourselves, how do we see the role we play? In method-acting classes, to understand a character the actor plays, they try to establish the root cause why the character does what he does. We have to do the same thing, establish the root cause determining why we do what we do, the reason we do what we do.

How do we decide to do what we do, do we give it any thought or do we just act? There is a difference between an improvisation and a script. Improvisation is more spontaneous, no written text to follow, it does not necessarily refer to a prescribed moral code. Do we have a written code which influences our actions or do we merely improvise, do we have restrictions on the actions we participate in, restrictions on the audience we invite, the people we associate with? Do we have restrictions on conversation, do we talk about everything or holy things? Where is our attention, who wrote our script, do we merely improvise?

Before we can improvise meaningfully we need to learn how to act. First we follow the script then we can improvise on it, first we learn the difference between right and wrong if we want to follow the path to God. Conscience does not develop immediately, wisdom does not come in the blink of an eye. There must be growth, appropriate action and learning. The prophet Muhammad said we should go all the way to China if we have to for wisdom. We must participate in the acquisition of wisdom. Once we learn the textual difference between right and wrong, the specific difference between right and wrong, we can improvise, then we will know whether what we are doing is right, we have established understanding, we have established the wisdom of conscience.

Now we understand limits and restrictions, we understand what is appropriate and we stay there. We will probably continue to act appropriately, but there is always a susceptibility to our lower self whose voice can steer us off the path. Our consciousness must guard against all the inner and outer forces trying to pull us from the truth, relentless forces which never give up. Since we will encounter them we do have to face them, we have to be as relentless as they are, or we succumb to their attacks. These attacks are not always straightforward, they can be subtle, disguised by something quite rational, they can use reason to lead us off the path.

Words have power, but they are nothing without our acts. Many people talk a good game without knowing how to play, and this playacting is the most important game we have, it is the act of our life. Either we fall into the passage of time as our life is eaten away, or we escape from the world and open the door to reality where time has no meaning, where we are no longer attached to the ravages of the world because our act is performed in reality. Our intention should be fixed on that timeless place, it should be fixed on that timeless One who has no beginning or end. We are no longer interested in the world of limits, the world which has a beginning and end.

Although our focus is on the limitless, our action must still be appropriate in the world of limits. God created the world of limits and He is merciful to it; if we are to be with Him we must also be merciful. To develop appropriate action here which will take us to the place beyond limits, we begin by understanding who we are, why we do what we do. We can think of ourselves as a blank slate on a blank stage, creating a play, a play which is our life. Who do we want to be in it, how do we want to act in it, does it matter what we wear, does it matter whether we wear the clothes of a pauper or a king? What is the important part of our act, what is important in reality, being rich or having gratitude? Do we understand the difference? If we have a bowl of watered down soup and we are grateful we have touched reality, if we have all the wealth of the world and we want more we have dug a grave.

We should understand the qualities which belong to God and those which belong to the world, then shift our focus to those which belong to God. Once we do that we realize that costume and titles, all the worldly things we see with our eyes, they are the least important part of the act. What is important is what lies behind all that, what is important goes on inside the actors, their focus, what they focus on. Who and what are we focused on, how do we achieve our goal? We need to pray about our focus and goals, we need to understand that patience is the umbrella of God's throne. While we are going from Act One to Act Two, or from Act Two to Act Three, what protects us from the anxiety of not being in the next act yet, or the anxiety of things not going exactly the way we want them to, that is one of God's qualities, patience.

Patience is the ability to sit without anxiety when things do not go the way we think they should, patience teaches us to look less at the way we think things should be and understand the way they really are. Perfection exists all around us. God did not create imperfection, but we are not always capable of seeing perfection. To discover who we really are we need the patience to discover that perfections exists, we need the patience to acquire the capacity for this. God is our ultimate audience. We pray that our actions in this world are appropriate for Him.

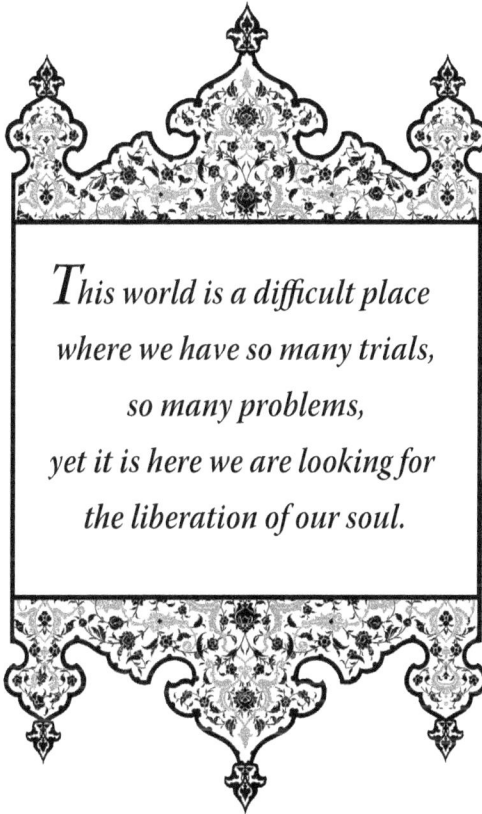

This world is a difficult place
where we have so many trials,
so many problems,
yet it is here we are looking for
the liberation of our soul.

The Paradox of Liberation

What the wise teachers have taught is a subtle teaching which requires subtle understanding. We are told we need to find liberation, the freedom of our soul, but to find this freedom we have to be bound in certain ways, we have to be bound to find our freedom. This world is a difficult place where we have so many trials, so many problems, yet it is here we are looking for the liberation of our soul. We encounter people who treat us unkindly, who treat us unfairly, who mock or deride us, who cause us difficulty, and still we are bound to forgive them, to find that liberation we are bound to forgive them. If we cannot understand this forgiveness, if we do not realize how we are bound to be forgiving, liberation cannot be ours.

We have duties in this world which means we have to find jobs, we need to be successful in the world. Nevertheless, when we are successful, people can be jealous of our success, but we are bound to our duty and bound to liberation, we have to do both. Sometimes if we are kind, generous and good to people, we are accused of acting with ulterior motives, people say there must be a reason why we are kind, generous and good, they do not understand that searching for liberation means we are bound to be kind, good and generous. Sometimes when we are honest and sincere in our dealings with people, they might think they can cheat us, in fact, they might, yet we are bound to be honest and sincere whether people treat us correctly or not, whether they cheat us or not.

The world is full of paradox; we feel inclined to react as others react to us, while we are bound to behave in the specific ways we understand to be our duty. If we are truly looking for liberation we have to understand the rules of this path, we have to understand how narrow this path we have to walk is, and not stray from it. Those who interfere with our state of being as we try to do what we are supposed to do is not what this is about, this is not about ourselves and others, it is only about ourselves and Him. When we constantly shift our focus to them, no matter who or what they are, our liberation is interrupted.

In our understanding of this we still have to do all that we need to do, and do it correctly, within the bounds of the permissible. Without the appropriate foundation there is no liberation, without the understanding of right and wrong, the adherence to what is permissible, liberation is unattainable. Things in this world are confusing and subtle. The world tells us we can do anything we want, we are free. Now we live here in Philadelphia, a rather free place, where we are free to engage in almost any activity we can think of as long as it is within the bounds of what is permitted by law, but does doing any of this give us freedom? What is freedom, what does our sense of freedom mean, what does it feel like, what does it really come from?

Philosophers talk of different kinds of utopia, they write about freedom in the world, peace in the world. One of the great lies was communism, the promise of freedom through economic equality, we would have our utopia in economic equality. What kind of freedom is it if we cannot say what we think, if we cannot work where we want, if the government does not allow us our relationship with God? When we cannot put our relationship with God into practice, when we do not have a relationship with God, is that any kind of freedom or is it merely being bound to the hypnotizing attractions of the world? We should be able to understand the subtle difference, understand what it is like to be hypnotized, to be asleep, to fall off the true path believing we are free. We should know whether we are actively engaged in our liberation or in our destruction, and recognize the difference.

This is not something which happens on the outside, this does not happen between someone else and us, it happens entirely within our own state of being. Teachers of truth and wisdom talk about it as the ability to remove ourselves from the lights, the fascination, the magnetic, hypnotic attractions of the world, and go to that inner world of peace where God exists. If God does not exist within, in our own heart, He does not exist for us; He might exist for others, but He does not exist for us. We must establish that relationship between God and ourselves, it is the point of being here, the point of our coming here, the point of our life, the only peace we can know, the eternal peace which comes from an actual relationship with our Creator.

The world is not a monument to our existence, it is not the end of everything, it is only one phase of existence. We believe there is more than one world, there is the world of souls, there is this world and the next. When we lose sight of the transitory nature of this world and put all our attention on a passing state, we have lost sight of our complete itinerary. If our itinerary includes going to Florida and to Sweden, we should bring both warm weather clothing and clothing for cold weather too; if we forget clothing for one part of our itinerary and end up in Sweden with nothing but shorts and a tee shirt, we are in trouble. Since our travels consist of more than this world, if we prepare for this world alone we have made a fundamental mistake about existence—we are not prepared for the rest of the trip. We need to understand this other portion of our being, of our existence, and the journey we have to prepare for.

When we are given a blessing by an illumined being, what is the blessing? The blessing given is in terms of provision for us in this world and in the next world, sustenance in this world and liberation in the next. We should understand how to sustain ourselves in this world, fulfilling all the duties we have in the appropriate way, attentively, bound to them. We should also understand the obligation to our soul, the obligation to our Creator because the journey, the itinerary continues, we have to be ready for the next world.

Things which keep us tied to this world, which are monumental in this world, are of little significance in the next, but the things God binds us to in this world are monumental in the next. The ability to be calm, to be forgiving, to love others even when they do not love us, this is not about our relationship with them, it is about our relationship with God who loves everyone, who is patient enough to wait for them to love Him, He has all the time there is. We are part of His creation, we are part of His plan, we are part of Him, and we should act as He does within the confines of this ephemeral situation. The truly wise teachers give examples of the next world, examples of the qualities which transcend this transitional state, examples of what continues beyond here, what takes us to the next step on this trip we call our life. They tell us there is no need to fight with others, if we know what to do we can proceed, if not, they can direct us the right way.

We need discipline in our lives, we need to correct ourselves, take hold of our own existence. We are no longer babies, we are mature now and maturity entails responsibilities, responsibilities to others, to ourselves. The exercise of these responsibilities is a display of our maturity. Self-absorption, egoism, pursuing titles and status are a display of our immaturity, it is giving credence to this world as if it were permanent, not temporary.

These teachers are travelers, they do not stay in one place very long, they are hard to hold onto. If we want to travel with them we have to ask for help. If we ask them the way, they are ready to show us, but first we need to empty ourselves of everything we have established so far, we have to give up the beliefs of this world. Understand that we have swallowed such a quantity of beliefs we do not even recognize them—they are so entangled with our inner self we cannot separate them. Once we believed so strongly in this world; now slowly we begin to taste the lies of the world. There is still a lot of cleaning to do, this is our work, the washing, cleaning, the purification we are bound to. We are bound to purification, to acts which purify us. We have to wash and scrub correctly to be clean.

When we polish others we also polish ourselves. Understand that when we forgive each other we are forgiven, when we give we are given, when we love we are loved. We create our own dynamic through this dynamic with others, something we must work on with great gentleness, kindness and love, binding ourselves to it, not wavering from it. This is the reason we are given a community, all the difficult people give us an opportunity to practice.

If we want to ascend to the next step on this path we need to be in the appropriate state for admission. We have heard these illumined teachers talk about their insignificance, describing themselves as tiny as an ant, and we understand this means they can go into places others cannot. Only the finest particles can pass through a filter, we should become these finest particles, clarify ourselves to be such fine particles. God's love helps us do this work; the more we are committed to this love, the less we worry about the people and things of the world, the more significant are the changes which occur. We no longer need the things we used to need, we are no longer bound to the world in the same way because we are bound to Him. The more we are bound to Him the greater our liberation.

May each of us understand this and choose to be bound to Him. May He grant us the glory, the love, the kindness and grace which are His to grant, the compassion, mercy and loving kindness which are His to give, the balm which soothes our hearts, our state of being. May we do His work in a state which is compassionate, merciful, kind and loving enough to represent Him.

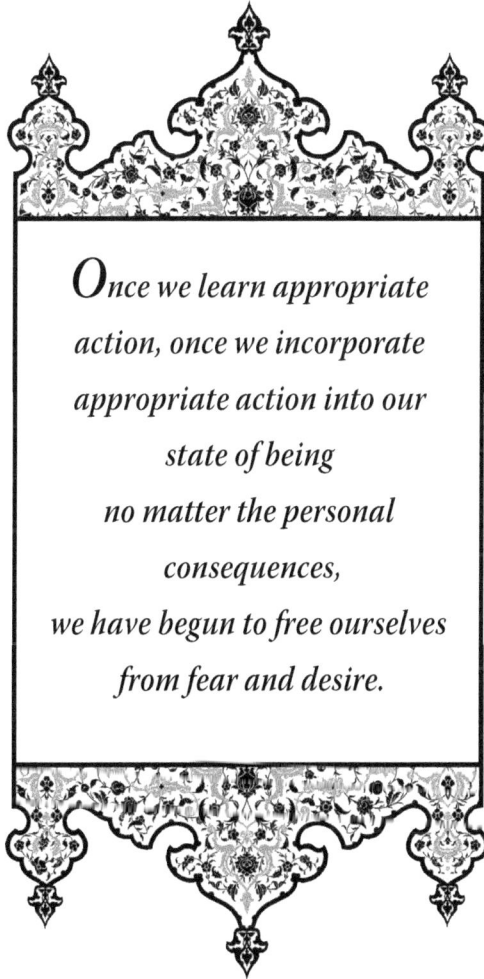

*Once we learn appropriate
action, once we incorporate
appropriate action into our
state of being
no matter the personal
consequences,
we have begun to free ourselves
from fear and desire.*

CHAPTER NINETEEN

Fear and Desire

Scripture tells us we must take refuge in God from the mischief caused by the presence of evil, the whisperer who withdraws. Who is this whisperer, what does he tell us and why, why does such a being exist? Where is he, how does he manifest and interact with us? We need to ask these questions because we are told we need to ask God for help, for protection from this presence. Let us think about an answer to these questions. Everything which exists on the outside exists on the inside. We should learn that our friends can elevate our life or destroy it. This tells us something about the whisperers on the outside, we need to be careful about those we associate with, but we should remember the whisperer does not exist only on the outside. Everything which exists outwardly also exists inwardly, we have something inside us we need to be protected from, something we take with us wherever we go.

Some people confuse the whisperer with themselves, thinking that what goes on in their minds is the self talking to the self. They do not realize truth and the nature of the mind, the truth of the lower self, the animal self; they do not realize we have two aspects, an animal self and an elevated self, one part stopping at intellect, the other going beyond.

Some philosophical systems suggest that both good and evil come from the mind, but this is not what we learn on this path: evil comes from the mind, good comes from God, and God is not our

153

mind. There is a difference here we should consider, we need to be cautious about the whisperers and our reaction to them. If we are in touch with our inner self, not merely reacting to the words and all the images which present themselves, we know the difference between being awake and asleep, being conscious and unconscious, reacting to truth and reacting to outer stimuli.

What pushes us, what pulls us, why are we pushed and pulled? If we are subject to fear of punishment or to our desires, we are subject to the whisperer who uses our attachment to that fear or these desires, pulling us away from truth. Without fear and desire the influence of the whisperer is diminished, its strength is diminished. The whisperer comes in many forms, in many manifestations. The whisperer can be a friend, a colleague, the whisperer can also be the animal qualities within ourselves, it can be a worldly demon leading us astray, it can be television or someone enticing us to commit some inappropriate act. Everything which pulls us away from truth, which pulls us away from God, is that whisperer.

We should be cautious about the things we hear, cautious about the things we see, the things we say, the places we go. When we are not careful we are subject to the whisperer. Why do we allow ourselves to see certain things, hear certain things, read certain things? We do this because we have certain desires—recognize the things we hold onto that we should let go of, come to the point when it is time to be rid of the things we need to be rid of. As long as we are satisfied with the way we are there is no progress, we are standing still, we remain the same. If our path is to be transformed, to become the being He wants us to be, if this is our intention we must know the truth about ourselves, make the effort to assess ourselves correctly, exactly, and have the courage to face who we are at this point in our life.

When we begin the judging process it is ourselves we judge, not others, we evaluate ourselves. Remember the story of Rābiʿah who said she did not want God because she feared hell or because she wanted heaven. Understand what this means, she wanted to be free of fear and desire, she did not want her relationship with God to be the same as her relationship with the world. She did not want fear and desire to rule her life, her life with God. There is an eleventh-century text which gives us an explanation of this. We are told that in the first century of Islam, Muslims treated each other with an understanding of their religion, meaning their way of life. When the understanding of religion grew thin they treated each other on the basis of loyalty to each other. As loyalty began to disappear they treated each other with religious chivalry, that is with correct, appropriate action. As appropriate action disappeared their treatment of each other was derived from a sense of shame, feeling embarrassed and inappropriate. As that sense of shame disappeared their treatment of each other was dictated by a desire for heaven and the fear of punishment.

If we interact with those we are close to on the basis of what we want from them or what we fear from them, what does this say about the level of interaction? We are at the animal level of desire and fear. What pulls us up from that level? Shame can change us, can alter us. If we understand what we have done was inadequate and wrong, then feel remorse, we can move to the next step. But if we have no shame, if shame has disappeared from our life, if the ability to understand we are wrong disappears, there can be no correction, there is no reason for correction, no red flag saying stop, something is wrong here.

We need an inner monitor to determine what we do; we should monitor our intentions, be aware of our intentions, know the reason why we do things, know what pushes us, what pulls us. When we are ashamed we realize our actions are inappropriate, we can begin to learn the difference between right and wrong, the first step on the path. This is religious chivalry, acting appropriately, doing what is right. We take the time to learn what is correct and what is incorrect.

Once we learn appropriate action, once we incorporate appropriate action into our state of being no matter the personal consequences, we have begun to free ourselves from fear and desire. Now we are no longer afraid of worldly consequences and no longer intent on producing specific results in the world, we are intent on being appropriate. As we behave appropriately over a period of time we develop loyalty to appropriate behavior, loyalty to our fellow beings. Then we do things with the recognition of love, the recognition of God within us all. We do no harm because we understand love, we understand God within us, we have loyalty to God's creation, loyalty to God's way, loyalty to the reason we are here.

Now we are close, we draw near the truth, God shows us His way. When we exist in that truth our will no longer manifests, our will disappears, we are empty of everything except His will. When we are empty there is no one home to listen to the whisperer, no one home to experience desire or fear, the things we need to disengage. Understand how this works, be a student, have the courage to look at the faults and endure the pain our shame inflicts.

This is critical because people usually run away from pain and rationalize the shame. Suddenly we find so many reasons why what we did was acceptable. Stare hard at the truth and accept its reality, know that change is possible, that change does occur, eliminate fear and doubt with faith in the truth. This is remorse, atonement, undertaking not to do that wrong thing again. This is atonement, not doing it again, removing it from the things we do. We all have categories of actions we engage, we all have lines we cross or do not cross, and each of us knows what they are. If we do not find all these lines appropriate yet, use the lines for the things we know we will not do. Understand the point when we know we will not go any further, then apply this recognition to the other things we do. Develop techniques to assist us on this path of transformation, recognize our faults and do something about them. Do not function in this world with fear of punishment or desire, go on the path of truth for the sake of truth. There is no access to truth with fear or desire.

There is no compulsion in religion, fear is compulsion. We cannot be moved to truth by compulsion, it is not possible. God tells us it does not work this way, it works because of change. Let us pray to change, let us ask those we have hurt or offended for forgiveness, let us ask God for forgiveness. Ask for forgiveness, act correctly, act with loyalty, act in God's way, the truth of existence. May the veils be lifted from us so that truth becomes evident and that which is inappropriate becomes abhorrent. May God make this clear.

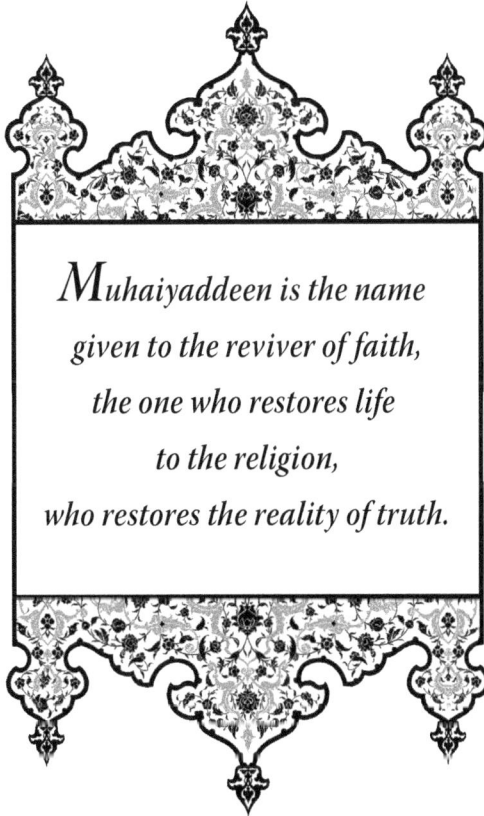

*Muhaiyaddeen is the name
given to the reviver of faith,
the one who restores life
to the religion,
who restores the reality of truth.*

CHAPTER TWENTY

Muhaiyaddeen

Muhaiyaddeen is the name given to the reviver of faith, the one who restores life to the religion, who restores the reality of truth. Muhaiyaddeen is the one who comes to us as the dīn, a life of truth, the one who comes as the living embodiment of the word. Some among us were blessed to have had Muhaiyaddeen, the living embodiment of truth, in our presence. When the being who has brought us the truth has to leave, those who try to perpetuate this reality do not understand its meaning if they do not become the meaning.

The difference between the prophet Muhammad and those who came after him was that Muhammad was the Qur'an, those who came after him merely read the Qur'an. There is a difference lying between being and reading. To understand what we witnessed means understanding what we have to become, we have to stop reading the Qur'an and start becoming the Qur'an. Muhaiyaddeen means understanding the book can be alive, it can be embodied; we have to see that embodiment and realize its possibility. Those who witnessed the possibility of what can exist must tell what happened, what does not stop happening, they must affirm it continues to happen, God does not abandon us. What happened before will happen again, and most important for each of us, it can happen within ourselves.

This does not mean all we have to do is sit around waiting for it, expecting it. We are told that God loves effort, it is up to us to make the effort. We might have had moments of inspiration, of overwhelming awe, gifts which God has given us, but we also have to work towards that state. It is interesting, hard to describe, to define, and just as hard to understand. To understand a state when we have not been in it is difficult. Without knowing algebra we cannot solve algebraic problems, but once we know algebra we have a method. Methodology and states of being are not the same thing, but they offer an analogy.

They say if we truly understood the first commandment, we would love God with our total being, but since we do not understand the total splendor of its meaning, we have to create this love for God and our fellow beings within ourselves. How do we do this? One reason for the existence of Bawa Muhaiyaddeen was to let us see how this can be done. We went to see the holy man to see how the Qur'an lives, how the embodiment acts. By watching his actions we could learn to imitate them, learn to act appropriately, learn what appropriate means. We start with knowledge, we are told things, told what to do, a primer, like a book for children. This is a study for children, in the spiritual state we are all children.

A wise person does not teach a child something inappropriate, saying never mind, he will get it right when he is older; he does not tell a child something incorrect or wrong to get through a difficult moment. Yet this is what our parents did, they told us inappropriate, misleading things when we were young, and now as adults we are trying to unwrap what they wrapped around us, every wrong thing from the time we were babies. We suffer because of this. We ourselves should always teach the truth to children or adults in the best way they can understand. This is what Bawa Muhaiyaddeen did, he taught us the truth in the best way we could understand. Sometimes people would ask a question which he answered, when they did not like the answer they would say he did not understand what they meant. Then he would repeat his answer, but they would say the translator made a mistake, and yet he would give the same answer again. This might happen several times until Bawa Muhaiyaddeen would end by saying, do whatever you want to do.

This was merely a polite way to say the conversation was over. They could not hear what he said, did not recognize he was guiding them to the appropriate answer. There was no compulsion in this, when they insisted they did not want the appropriate way, he would say do what you want.

Do we hear the right answer and still do what we want, does our mind tell us we can do what we want, we have a dispensation? When some meet a holy man they believe they have a special dispensation: in the company of a holy man they are somehow holy too. They translate what they see as something that is theirs, just as the mind translates what is said to let them do what they want.

We have to understand who we are, understand our state, but it is difficult to monitor ourselves, difficult to understand our state. Sometimes we mistranslate our feelings to protect our sense of self. Sometimes, when we are jealous we do not recognize our jealousy, we call it an appropriate reaction to someone else's arrogance, we blame them. Then when we are arrogant we do not call it arrogance, we are self-righteous, merely doing what is correct to uphold a principle, we are protecting others from themselves. The truth is we need to protect ourselves from ourselves, there is no righteousness in the self, righteousness exists with God alone. When we understand this we worry less about ourselves and being righteous, then we can catch sight of a higher understanding. As long as we are busy defending every move we make, defending ourselves against everyone around us, we become defenders of God, not lovers of God, there is a difference. Those who defend believe they love, they think they are defending love and truth.

Gandhi once said, "I used to think God is the truth, but I've learned that the truth is God." We automatically practice the system of faith we were taught as a child, even if we know it is somehow wrong. And we call that God, we call that truth, but unless it soothes the heart with love, unless it is appropriate no matter the interpretation, it is not the truth, it is not God. Those who do understand the truth can become something like a walking scripture, a correct interpretation in appropriate action. This sort of holy text does not require words from those who behave inappropriately, whose words are nothing more than shouting. Consider how absurd it is for people to assume they are protecting God, that God needs us to protect His word, His way. If God wants things a certain way they are as He wants them. He needs us to imitate Him as best as we can, He needs us to allow others the freedom to understand Him, to imitate Him as best as they can. We need the open space allowing each of us to do that.

This world is a dangerous place, there are some places where people are fortunate to live where there is no war, no killing, no famine, where people are permitted to live as they think is best, where there is tolerance. There are places in the world where the punishment for conversion, for choosing a different path is death, where religious conversion is not allowed, even talking about conversion is not allowed. Some live where there is tolerance for different ideas, sects and ways of doing things. Unfortunately, the whole world does not understand this, the world wants its own interpretation of things, it wants everyone to follow its own interpretation. When we are not in the right place, the true place, and we feel insecure, the only way to feel more secure is by forcing others to follow us, make them follow our beliefs, then when we see everyone doing what we do, we think we are right. Being right is not about numbers, if it were we would have millions of Muhaiyaddeens. If only one person in ten million is doing the right thing, what does that say about the others, what does it say about their arrogance, their state? Isn't it amazing that some think killing people is an appropriate way to believe in God?

We have to acknowledge this while we really concentrate on who we are, on our state, on the state of our love. How do we measure our state of love? One way to check our love is to notice the level of disdain for others, the ability to tolerate others, our reaction to others. If someone mistreats us what do we do? Once when Bawa Muhaiyaddeen was talking to God he asked, "Why have You sent me here God, everyone abuses me, everyone causes problems for me, why did You send me here?"

The response came, "Someone has to soothe their hearts, someone who can take the abuse and the slander but still love them on My behalf. Someone must do that, this is the reason I sent you here, they need someone who can show them this so that they will change."

Who are we, how do we interact with each other, with ourselves when we face a difficult place in our own state of being, when we face the embarrassment of the things we have done to others? Do we run away and hide, do we say enough of this, let's go back to everything is all right, or do we somehow work our way through it? Do we acknowledge our mistakes and ask for forgiveness, even if our mistakes horrify us? If we were abused as a child we may become an abuser because this is what we know. First we have to face the abuse we received as children, then we have to recognize that we passed along these inappropriate ways to others. The terrible thing done to us is what we do to others. It takes courage to face this, to ask for forgiveness, repent. Repent means not doing the same thing again.

If we pull these mistakes from the core of our being, if we annihilate our faults we can alter who we are. We cannot completely annihilate them, the lower self will be with us our whole life, we have to live with that lower self without paying attention to it, we have to keep doing what is appropriate. When the prophet Muhammad was asked if he still had a lower self, if he still had base desires, he answered yes, but he had made them believers, he had taught them to obey. He did not teach them to be exalted, he taught them to obey. We need to teach our base desires to obey, when they want to shout we say no as we would to a child. These desires function at the level of a child we have to keep in the right place, we have to make the child understand it cannot be allowed to dominate our consciousness, it cannot be the driving force of our existence or tell us what to do.

Muhaiyaddeen is the one who brings life to the dīn, the path, the way, the one who brings light to faith, who brings life to the true life within us, our higher self, to the true being hidden by the lower self. Muhaiyaddeen revives our soul to give it the strength to deal with the world. We need Muhaiyaddeen in our life, we need to bring to life what actually is life, not its imitation which is illusion. Muhaiyaddeen does away with illusion, bringing reality into existence. Reality exists within us, it is part of us. We are meant to live the reality, but the billions of hypnotic fascinations alive in the world prevail in our mind.

The mind is so obsessed with the trivia of the world it cannot see the larger picture, it cannot see who we are. There are no solutions to be found in all the obsessive trivia, they offer nowhere to go, there is no end to this, there is no correcting this. There is a flaw in that system which cannot be removed, that system which does not have God. Only when God is brought into our understanding of things, only when we recognize Him as the only existent thing can we remove ourselves from illusion. As long as we think we can find solutions with any understanding other than there is no god but God, God alone exists, we have no solution, we have degradation and inappropriate thinking. So much of this inappropriate behavior has been called normative by society, acceptable, so much has been reinforced by those who behave this way that it is not only seen to be right, anyone who does not is considered abnormal.

We have to live with separation from many things, we have to live with being unaccepted, live with being pushed away. We must not be sad about this, instead we should learn to love, with love we can conquer not being loved. This path is not about our needs, it is about our ability to do certain things, about our ability to become. It is not about what we will get from others, we cannot get anything from them, only God can give us what we need. The more we understand this and focus on it, the more it satisfies us, the more love we have, the more we taste the truth.

To go from one place to another we have to take a journey, if we do not set out we cannot know what happens on the way. Once we start the journey we understand there is somewhere to go. Muhaiyaddeen is the place to go, Muhaiyaddeen is the answer to so many things. We were told by Muhaiyaddeen to be Muhaiyaddeen. He said, "Be like me." How do we continue the teaching? By becoming the teaching. Shams of Tabriz threw all of Rūmī's books into the water because Rūmī had to be the books, he had to become the truth. This is the reason why Muhaiyaddeen came, he came to say the truth exists in being, he showed us how to look into the mirror of becoming.

We ask God to make Muhaiyaddeen visible, to make this mirror bright enough for us to understand the nature of the state we call Muhaiyaddeen. May we imitate that and become that ourselves.

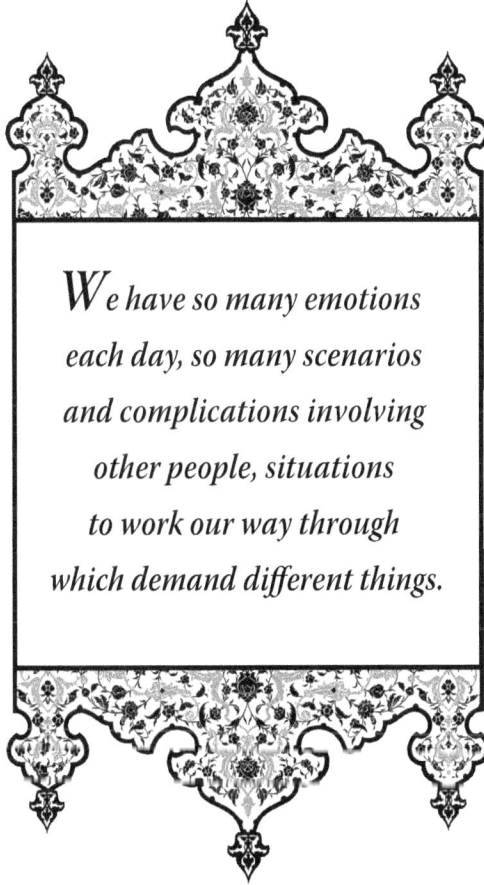

We have so many emotions each day, so many scenarios and complications involving other people, situations to work our way through which demand different things.

Letting Go

We have so many emotions each day, so many scenarios and complications involving other people, situations to work our way through which demand different things. There are times in our life when we think the most important thing is to have friends, times when we think the most important thing is to have money, have the right partner, times when the most important thing is to be famous, to have power. Each of these needs drives us in a particular way. We should be aware of our needs, how they drive us, be aware of the emotions they provoke and our reaction to these emotions. We should understand the importance we place on these needs, understanding as well the reality of their importance in our life. Are they really important or not? To make this assessment we need a perspective on existence.

Let us consider what our life is about, take a moment to understand that without any of those needs actually being fulfilled we are still here, we still exist. Let us think about the freedom we have when we let go of them, the ability to sit in peace when we let them go. If we can sit in peace by letting them go, why don't we do this? What makes us so emotionally fragile, so overcome, overwhelmed, distraught, angry, fearful? What makes us behave this way, why do we react, how do we become less vulnerable, what allows us peace?

We are vulnerable in so many ways; when we hear someone

say something about us we shudder, even if it's a lie something inside us shudders. Why does this happen? Why are we affected by words which are not true, why do we react to a need to influence others, why do we need to be liked, to be famous, to have power? Why do we need these things, what is missing in us that needs all this? Quite simply, love is missing. We think we'll have love with power, with fame, we think we'll have love when our friends give us their approval. When we are empty we look for love in all these places. We need love because it heals us, but we are looking in all the wrong places, we must learn how to find it within ourselves, we must learn how to generate love from within ourselves. Generating love means figuring out how to find it in ourselves, how to have love flow through us, it means figuring out the process.

How do we find enough love to fill the emptiness we sometimes try to fill with friends, with acceptance, money, power, fame, drugs, alcohol, all the addictions of the world? First we have to be in touch with our own experience, remembering those moments when we were at peace. We have all had such moments, if we are really honest we will find they were not because of money, power, fame or acceptance. They occurred in a situation of unconditional love, when no one was pushing us and no one was pulling us, no one wanted anything from us, we were satisfied with everything exactly as it was. There was no reason to rush away, there was nowhere to go, we were already where we wanted to be, there was nothing we needed.

The satisfaction at that moment did not rise because we had all the outer things we needed, this satisfaction was not about external things. That moment came because we were in a state of inner equilibrium, the need for external things had left us, the need for satisfaction from external things had left, we were satisfied with the equilibrium from letting things go. When we had let go of the things we thought we needed there was room for God's love, we were not trying to fill ourselves with all that outer stuff which cannot, in any case, be placed within. This letting go is something we need to practice, we need to understand how to do it if we are to understand our life, understand how to relieve ourselves of trauma and turmoil. Consider the fear some people have because they worry about what others think, the fear some people have because of a specific problem, consider the emotional trauma collected over the years by some as they try to make their situation coincide with what others consider normal.

Science has found they can predict behavior statistically but not individually, they can predict the percentage of people who will survive with a certain treatment, but not which individuals. Subatomically, they can say that half a certain amount of radium will disappear in sixteen hundred years because the atoms are unstable, they fly off, but they cannot say which atoms will stay and which will go. They can give a statistical idea of what will happen, but they cannot be specific about individual particles. Is it better to go or better to stay, better to be within the statistical norm of what stays or better to be something that cannot be measured? What cannot be measured, what is so outside the statistical norm that no one sees it, no one understands it, touches it, feels it, no one can count it, write it down or draw its pictures? Who is trying to imitate what we call this statistical norm, what we call normal behavior, what we see people do?

What are we trying to be part of, a measurable, statistical average or something that cannot be measured? What is our life about, things the newspapers can write about or something they cannot write about? Are we trying to be what is on television, or are we trying to be what television cannot show because they have no idea what it is? Are we trying to be the rituals of religion or are we trying to be the truth expressed in the rituals? Understand how to measure our life, understand how to be unafraid. Not being afraid is important. That part of us which shudders when someone talks about us reacts because we are afraid, afraid we will not be liked, afraid we will not be accepted. We need a perspective on existence, an understanding that reality cannot be measured, written or talked about, it can only be experienced.

Reality cannot be experienced for us by our friends and associates, we are the only ones who can experience it and be satisfied. We do not need to ask our friends if they are satisfied with our reality so that we can be at peace. When the last day comes we go by ourselves, anyone who has told us what to do, when and how to do it will not be there with us. We must have courage and be ready for that day. We need the courage to be unafraid when the time for our inner battle comes, and we need to be ready. There is an inner battle because the world keeps showing us things which make us fearful.

Imagine a circle and an arc on that circle. Now imagine that we are a spot on the arc, the only spot we know. We know a little about the arc but nothing about the rest of the circle—if we limit ourselves to the knowledge we have we limit who we can become. If we think the arc of the circle is the whole circle we have limited our existence; if we think we know what is going on all around us and what we know is all there is to know, we have limited our existence; if we think our mind can know all there is to know, we have thought ourselves out of reality and an experience of God.

We should know our limits, know that God will do away with those limits in His time when we are ready. We will be shown in His time, we must have that patience, that courage, and be ready for an inner fight when difficult times come. We do have to fight with ourselves, sit patiently through difficult times without reacting, being steadfast in faith. This is the path, this is our life, this is the search for reality. It is important to know whether this is what we are doing or not, and every once in awhile we should check, we do have a tendency to go to sleep, to forget where we are. There are no alarm clocks to wake us from this sleep, the only thing that wakes us is peace. When we are at peace we can recognize all the moments we are not at peace, we can see the difference. As long as we are overwhelmed by the pushing, the pulling and the trauma of the world we do not have time to be peaceful.

Whatever we concentrate on, whatever has traumatized us is what controls us. Physical disabilities are much more difficult than disabilities projected by the mind, but these mental traumas are serious. To heal our mental traumas, we have to use the tools taught by the saints. First, we have to realize traumas exist, second, we have to realize we are affected by them, and third, we have to recognize where they came from, how they caught us, and finally, we have to know how to heal ourselves.

May God put the cure in our hands, then may we cure ourselves and learn to help others.

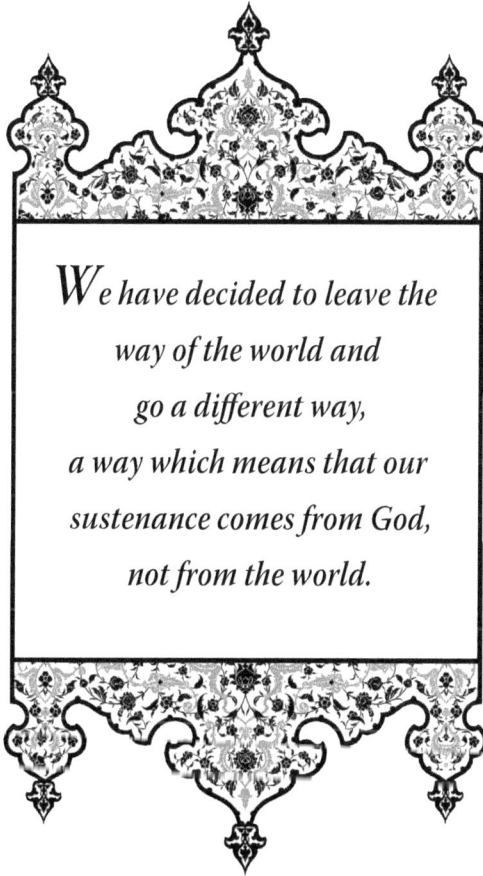

CHAPTER TWENTY-TWO

We have decided to leave the
way of the world and
go a different way,
a way which means that our
sustenance comes from God,
not from the world.

The Profit Motive

There is competition in this world as we work to earn a living, competition for money, competition in business and among those who are trying to sustain their material existence. This is the way of the world, a state of continuing competition. Little fish eat smaller fish and then they are eaten by bigger fish; everything is in competition with everything else for sustenance in the world. Capitalism includes the profit motive, we go out there for gain, that monetary gain which sustains ourselves and our family is permissible.

There is competition and there is the permissible within competition; in other words, as long as we function with integrity, we are encouraged to play the game of the world. Certain things are forbidden, high interest for instance, high interest which can destroy someone is not permitted. In capitalist competition usury is forbidden, although both competition and gain are permissible.

There is the path of the world and the path to God, the path of real human beings, true human beings who are not in competition with each other. The rules of capitalism do not apply to our dealings with each other. When we are competitive with each other, when our mind and our attitude insist we must prevail, difficulties arise. Some people not only need to do what they do, but they also need others to accept what they do and what they think. If this is a driving force in their life they can go astray on this great path.

We are here to love each other, not to force each other. Tolerance is an astonishing quality which we find in all the great teachers. We need to understand this quality in our dealings with each other, we need to understand the rules of the straight, true path because the rules of this path are different from the rules of the world. Even if the rules of the world, for the world, are permissible, they are not permissible in our dealings with friends and companions. We cannot be demanding of them, we cannot have separations among us, we cannot have competition among us. We need to be joyous in the joy of our friends and sad in their sorrow, we need to be deeply sympathetic to the lives of others.

We should practice the act of having no act, and that means we come without motive, without agenda, we come to serve others because we are without needs. God has provided for us, we are fortunate, we have seen His grace and know that everything we need has already been given to us. We are without needs because God has given us all that we need. Shouldn't we help those who still have needs, shouldn't we set the table for those who have needs? They have not understood that their needs are only products of their imagination, an imagination which requires feeding until they recognize they can be self-sustaining.

Let us understand what self-sustaining means: to be self-sustaining in truth means we are sustained by our true self. What is our true self? Our true self is our connection to God which alone sustains us, we need nothing else to sustain us. We have problems when we compete with friends and associates. If they say something we think is not quite right, if we feel we deserve praise which they do not give, if they blame us when we think they have no right to do so, all this causes trouble. We need to be impervious to praise and impervious to blame.

We do not take sustenance from the world nor do we take sadness from the world, happiness and sadness are not what the world has for us. We have decided to leave the way of the world and go a different way, a way which means that our sustenance comes from God, not from the world. Those who look for sustenance from the world need manifest indications of success, they need signs to persuade themselves they are happy, they need proof that what they are doing is correct if their faith is weak, if their belief is weak, they need proof that the world supports them. Looking for this proof, looking to the world for sustenance and indications of worthiness means we need the qualities of the world. What are the qualities of the world? They start with a deep sense of differences, the root of the problem as we look for success in the world.

If we look for success in the world, if we see differences, we create our own image of the way things ought to be; as soon as we take that and our own image seriously, we are in a forbidden realm. Now we have jealousy and resentment. If things are not the way we think they ought to be, we resent the people who are not the way we want them to be, we become jealous of their success which should be ours. Now we have engaged the things of the world, the things which make competition what it is, we add winning and losing to the equation of brotherhood and friendship where they do not belong. We have to bring a different understanding to brotherhood, keep score in an entirely different way. We are not in the business of competition, we are in the business of surrender, the opposite of competition. Competition means we win by overcoming someone else, surrender means we win by overcoming ourselves, the self disappears and God wins.

We need to understand this game of surrender, this act which must become the act of our lives. We are all actors and actresses, each of us has an act, and we do have to be careful about the one we choose. We are idol worshipers until we come to that point which is reality. We should be careful about what we worship, ask God to remove everything separating us from reality. Even though we might be aware of the separation between what we worship and reality, we have to pray for the separation to disappear.

We have been given examples of the truth, reality and the right way to live; we should model ourselves on that reality. We have the example of the prophets, the example of enlightened teachers, of all the friends of God. We know what they went through, the suffering they endured on behalf of others. The profit motive must disappear in our interaction with each other, we do not acquire profit from each other. If God permits it we acquire God from each other, God is our profit, God is beyond profit, a treasure which cannot be described. This is available if we leave the world to its own rules and establish new rules for ourselves. With God's help we will be allowed this, in our struggle with ourselves we will begin to understand the new way, the path of surrender which is the only way to approach Him, the only way to cleanse ourselves, be worthy of approaching Him.

This path begins very simply, it starts in our home, it starts in our relationship with our husband or wife, it expands to the relationship with our children, then to the relationship with our companions in fellowship. That relationship of love, of kindness, striving for the sake of others, happiness in doing things for others, this is the path we have chosen, the path our great teachers chose. Think about their profit motive, think how they kept score, what they intended and wanted. They never took anything for themselves, their intention was always to give, to elevate others.

We should help others, be the best parents to our children, help ourselves and everyone we know, all our friends and companions. We have to be the best friend we can be, the best example of sharing, of giving. We do not rush to talk about ourselves, we are happy to listen to someone else, we learn to have sympathy. We cannot help someone else unless we become who they are, we have to be there, share everything with them and let them in, then we can react on their behalf.

A sage dealt with a certain situation in an interesting way. It seems a mother came to him asking for help with her child—she wanted him to stop eating sugar. The wise man told the woman in question to come back in two or three weeks. When the woman returned with her child, he told the child to stop eating sugar. The mother asked, "Why did you make us wait for you to say that?"

The answer was, "First I had to stop eating sugar, I had to understand what the child would experience and know how it felt." We need to understand what other people are experiencing, walk in their shoes, take ours off. We cannot be so attached to our own shoes we have no time to step into someone else's.

If we believe everything needs to proceed as we think it should, we have taken a step which is impermissible, we are creating the world as we think it should be, and we do not have that right. We have the right to help, the right to assist, the right to use good qualities, we have the right to disappear, but we do not have the right to judge or insist. This path is difficult because it runs against the self-preservation everyone assures us is a driving force. What good does it do to preserve the body if we lose the soul? This is not new, we have heard this before, but now we need to understand the truth of it.

These old maxims embody the reality of our lives; we need to cling to the reality of our lives, tune into things which keep us right, make us clear, united with others. We should share ourselves freely and easily, not only our goods but ourselves as well. We have to make ourselves available to all those who want something from us, and we should not see it as a burden, we should see it as an opportunity to do His will. Our purpose is to help, the hand which helps is the path we have been taught. It must be the path we choose.

Choosing this path means we have to understand its rules, its requirements, we have to understand the inner cleansing process of the path. Every motive except for His qualities must disappear. Any other motive means we need to keep washing ourselves again and again, like Shakespeare's Lady Macbeth who tried to remove the stain of her inhumanity by washing her hands obsessively. We need to remove the stain of the world.

We do have to be careful on this path because there are people who cannot be helped, people we should not try to help. We must not impose ourselves, imposing ourselves on those who are obsessed with their own needs, their own way, will cause problems. If we throw a knife at a stone wall it bounces off, there is no receptivity. We should keep to people who are receptive, who want to be receptive. Those who do not understand can be taught if they choose, although those who do not understand but do not want to learn present a different situation. We have to distinguish among them without being naïve. We need to be brave, we need to be clear and act with wisdom.

Wisdom differentiates what we can and cannot do, what is available and what is not. Wisdom opens the path showing us how to extend ourselves, how to fulfill our responsibility to God. We still have this body, we still have old age, all the problems that come with being human, and we must be merciful, have the mercy which understands the limits of our own abilities while still doing all we can. We cannot accept the competitive path the world offers, we cannot have resentment, jealousy and anger, we cannot because that would be surrendering to the world.

Everybody serves someone. People who think they are in a competition have actually surrendered to darkness and evil. All the options have been laid out for people who have thought it through, they know where they are going; but so many have not thought it through, perhaps because they are frightened when they look at themselves too closely. We have to pass through this frightening stage when we see ourselves and feel ashamed of what we have done, what we have experienced, ashamed of what we did and who we are. Yet we must also remember that God re-creates us with every breath, that the universe is not only created by God, it is also sustained by Him, sustained with every breath.

Opportunities come with every breath, opportunities continue as long as we breathe, each breath is a new opportunity to walk the path in the right way. We should feel it, know this as reality, pray for that understanding. If we do our prayers with this intention, each moment of intention takes us away from the self and closer to Him. God help us understand this path, this way, help us grow and be satisfied. May He grant our sustenance so that His love will fill us without needing anything from the world, may we not look for satisfaction from the world. We take our satisfaction from Him, we are sustained by Him alone.

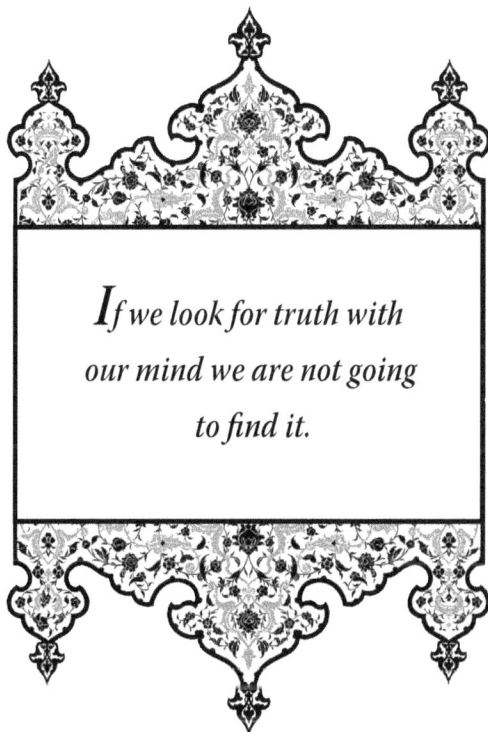

If we look for truth with our mind we are not going to find it.

Beyond the Mind

Traveling this subtle path to God means we have to go to places appropriate for the path, we cannot find things if we look in the wrong places. There is a story about a great sheikh, a teacher, who traveled from community to community. One day word spread through a certain city that he was coming. When a sheikh with a large following who lived there was told that a renowned sheikh was coming and that they should all visit him, he said, "If he sends me an invitation I will go to see him."

One student, devoted to his teacher, understood that such an invitation would probably not be forthcoming. He traveled to the next town to tell the itinerant sheikh about his own sheikh. Since his own sheikh would not come without an invitation, he asked to have one sent. The great sheikh looked at him, "Well, I'll send an invitation because you've asked, but know that your teacher is more interested in himself, his interest is focused on his beard. Even though that is so, I'll give you an invitation for him."

On the evening of their invitation there was a large gathering with the sheikh and all his disciples. Once the meeting finished the city sheikh stayed behind to meet the great sheikh who began to tell him the truth about himself. "You know, your focus is really yourself, actually, it is on your beard."

The city sheikh started to cry, "It's true, it's true!" ripping out his beard.

The great sheikh looked at the disciple who had asked for the invitation, "As I told you, he is focused on his beard."

We have to recognize what we are really focused on, understand where we are searching for truth. If we look for truth with our mind we are not going to find it. Looking with the mind is like putting water in a sieve—the mind is not a receptacle to hold the truth. Understand what the mind can and cannot do for us. When we say to our mind we want to be rid of every motive attached to ourselves, this is mind discussing mind. The mind has nothing but motives of the self, discussing this prospect with the mind only entrenches us more deeply in selfhood. When we discuss getting rid of self-motivation with our mind it does give us something to do, if that is what we are looking for, but if we are hoping to make progress we have to give it up, find another way. The other way is so obvious we miss it, to be rid of these motives we involve ourselves with other people, we help others for their sake, in a way which has nothing to do with ourselves. This is a simple, direct approach.

Many of us understand only half the golden rule, we do not understand reciprocity, a process which works two ways: do unto others as you would have them do unto you. Generally, people are interested in what others do for them, how others treat them, what they are getting from them. Most of us forget the other half, how are we with others, how do we act towards others, what are we doing on their behalf, how are we treating them? There is a lot of work to do if our regret boils down to self-flagellation, to pulling out our beard, it means we are still deeply interested in ourselves, we have not been able to dislodge this obsession. We need to understand the bag of bones we walk around in, we need to release ourselves from both the physical prison and the mental prison attached to the bag of bones. If we are incapable of doing this we are merely marking time instead of doing what we must do. If we use our mind to read all the books about becoming something else, nothing happens.

Most of us do not know how to function without our mind, we are afraid to let it go, we have been told to memorize things, to learn things, repeat them. What is it we use to do all that? We use our mind, we have learned how to use our mind. Those who are most successful have the greatest difficulty going beyond the mind because they have been rewarded with titles, honors, degrees and awards, acquired by its use. How do we make the break and release ourselves from this life we are accustomed to, for many of us it is the only way we know how to be, so how do we do that? It takes a certain courage, a belief that something else is going on, something beyond ourselves. We all talk about God, we talk about God creating us, sustaining and nourishing us. We say it is up to God, everything is in His hands, but how many of us believe it, how many of us believe everything is in God's hands?

There is a story about a disciple who wanted to show his teacher he truly believed everything was in God's hands. He put on sackcloth and sat down where the caravans drove by, holding up his beggar's bowl. As the caravans went by people gave him money. He went back to his teacher, "I gave up my job, I gave up everything and dressed like a beggar. Look what God has given me."

The teacher replied, "Interesting, but dress like a prince, go to a place where no one walks by. Let's see if God provides for you. Do you have enough courage to do that?"

The disciple was confused, he had gone into a different kind of business, the beggar's business, he had confused his beggar's business with not being in business at all, even taking the proof to his teacher. He persuaded himself he was doing something else although he was still working with his mind. How do we give up our dependence on the mind and go into the open space where it does not affect us? We must believe that God exists, we really need to believe it and understand that. It is not the mind's determination which makes something happen. Nothing happens without God allowing it.

It has been easier for me to believe it because my experience has proved it for me, has taught me to think about things in a different way. I used to think I could accomplish things because I was clever, but my entrepreneurial enterprises taught me something else. I am no more or less clever from one enterprise to the next, yet some work out and some do not. What makes some work and others fail? Clearly not myself or they would all work out. I soon realized it had nothing to do with me; God allows some things and does not permit others. With this understanding I no longer think I am clever, I realize that what I receive comes from His grace. Now I feel gratitude, I do not feel clever. This is an alteration in consciousness, a different approach, a different attitude which has nothing to do with what we can or cannot do. God only has to say, "Be!" and it happens, we've been told this. We believe whatever God wills happens. If everything is dependent on His will, what is left for us? We have been told that our intention and our patience are left to us.

This then, is not about what happens or how things turn out. It is not about what we can see. Do we see intention? This is not about what we go through to comprehend these things, it concerns what we intend, it concerns our patience with the process, watching our intention and keeping it focused correctly no matter the hardships trying to cancel it. This is a combination of the intention and our patience to see it through, this is not about results.

Culture is about results, understanding that this is not about results turns our culture which is entirely about results upside down. At work we are expected to give reports on what we have done, results are expected. In our friendships there is sometimes the unspoken question, what have you done for me lately? Instead, we should try to understand God's blessing is all there is to ask for. This means a shift in attitude, a shift in who we are, a different way of looking at things. This means we find our excitement in different places, we have gratitude for different things, our peak experiences come from different sources. For some, peak experiences are making a lot of money and buying expensive things. We measure our life with the things we think elevate us, enhance us, the things we think make us better.

What does actually make us better? One tradition summarizes all our misconceptions as reliance on earth which is property, on gold which is wealth, and on sensual gratification or pleasure, the very things we need to learn to do without. It must be something else, what tells us we are in the midst of an extraordinary moment, an extraordinary experience? This comes from watching an appropriate intention come to fruition. If we have the intention to be filled with flowing love and we see that happen, if we feel this love which is part of us spread to others and that is our peak experience, we are changed, altered, we have learned not to measure with our mind. If the smile of a baby is a peak experience, if it reverberates truth, freedom and God's existence in the world we have begun to change.

This understanding is connected to God, to His gracious qualities, to making these qualities part of who we are. When we see the relationship to God and His qualities as the most important relationship in our life we know change has begun. These qualities are not just for ourselves, when they exist within us they spread to everyone close by. We understand these questions have no boundaries, they are not bound up within ourselves, they pass right through us. While we remain in a state which allows these things to pass through us, we can direct them to places where they are needed. God permits them to flow through us if we have emptied ourselves of self; He alone exists. This is the state we strive for. We pray that He allows all of us to enter this state.

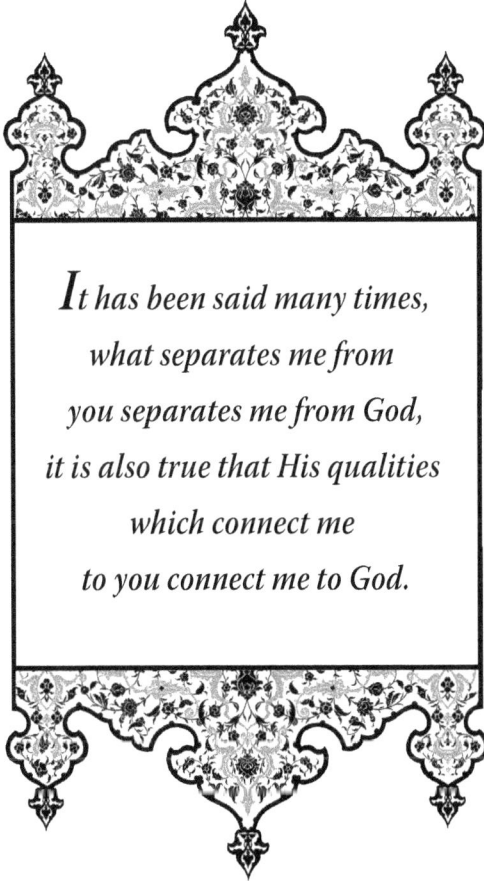

It has been said many times,
what separates me from
you separates me from God,
it is also true that His qualities
which connect me
to you connect me to God.

Brotherhood

Veterans of war understand the meaning of brotherhood. Sad that we have to give examples of war to show what brotherhood is like, even though we do need to understand what it means to defend each other, to make sacrifices for each other and be gracious. If we can do this there are certain rewards. What are the rewards? Who is the gracious One, the One who supports, protects and helps, who is the only real friend? When we behave with His qualities we share in Him, and when we share in Him He joins us, we have a taste of His grace because of our conduct and attitude towards each other, with His actions we heighten the experience of that divine resonance.

Selfish, jealous, divisive qualities work the opposite way, they separate us from each other. What separates me from you separates me from God, it is also true that His qualities which connect me to you connect me to God. If we want to be connected to God we must make the connection. If we are not connected we should recognize what we are failing to do. This is not complicated, it is quite basic, but we do sometimes miss these basic things.

It is important to interact with people appropriately, in a loving way, in a kind, gracious and positive way. Learning how to do this is the transformation we are talking about, a transformation teaching us how to interact with God. This path concerns our relationship with God. To be close to God we need to be close to those who are close to Him, the servant can introduce us to the Master. If we have the grace to meet such a servant, we have to learn how to behave with the servant, if we cannot behave correctly with the servant we will never come to the Master; the servant holds the key to His door.

There is a traditional story about Moses inviting God to a banquet. He prayed so hard for God to come that God answered Moses and said He would come. Days were spent in preparation, then just before the banquet was supposed to start a poor man came asking for bread and water. Moses, explaining how busy he was, asked him to come back later. The banquet began, many people came but there was no sign of God.

Later, when Moses was praying he said, "I asked You to come, You said you would, yet You did not."

God answered, "I came, I asked you for bread and water, but you said you were busy and sent me away."

Part of our interaction with God is connected to our interaction with His presence in the people we meet. We have an obligation to be consistently good to everyone; our initial obligation is to be gracious, loving and kind. When we sustain this, certain gifts are granted.

In so many religious institutions we find that a large part of their work is to protect the institution. Protecting the institution becomes the same as protecting God. Until we understand that God does not need our protection, that He alone is sufficient, that He takes care of every situation, until we have this trust and live its truth it is difficult to have appropriate relations with others.

We are each the totality of existence, we are the universe, each one of us. If the universe is to pour out patience we have to be the one pouring out patience, if the universe is to pour out generosity we have to be the one pouring out generosity, if the universe is to pour out love we have to be the one pouring out love. Otherwise, we interfere with the natural flow of things. To prevent this interference we must analyze our motives, analyze how they have been conceived then rationalized, analyze our basic assumptions.

Everything belongs to God. He does not need our protection, He is the protector in need of nothing from us, He is the One who bestows it all. Our duty is to defer to His will, to avoid interfering with His will. The glory of our existence lies in understanding this point, unless our assumptions are based on this principle we block the truth. If we think we have to protect a religious institution, if we think without our direct interference His words and the truth will fade, we have not understood His glory. His truth cannot fade, His truth is all that exists.

The teachings of the holy beings are like rain which falls everywhere. There is great joy for those who collect this rain. Unless we sustain this joy the rewards do not follow. As long as we confine ourselves to what we see, as long as we think sanctity is what can be seen, we miss the point.

Let us make each other joyful, let us help each other, rejoice in each other's success and be grateful in each other's presence. Then God is joyful for us, then all the veils melt away.

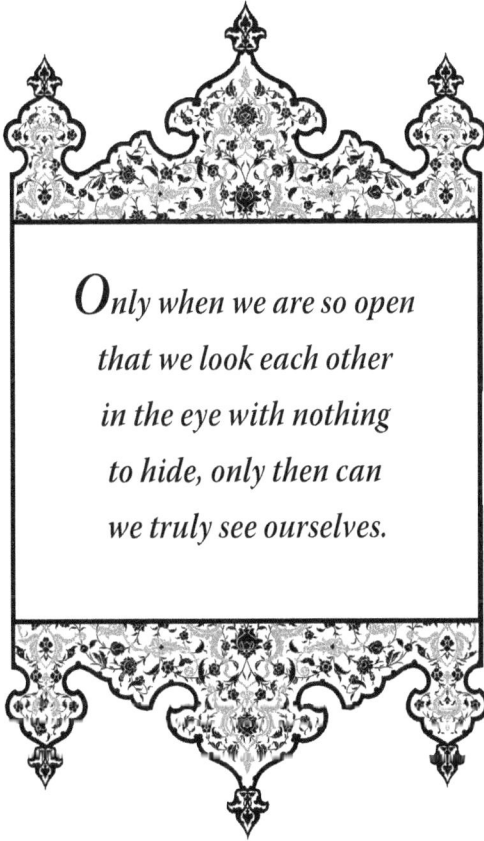

*Only when we are so open
that we look each other
in the eye with nothing
to hide, only then can
we truly see ourselves.*

CHAPTER TWENTY-FIVE

Hypocrisy

May the peace of God be with you, now and always. Sometimes as we develop from childhood to maturity we discover that certain actions will or will not get us what we want, and we learn how to adapt ourselves to situations so that we do get what we want. We learn to say what needs to be said to achieve our goals, we learn to manipulate, to lie, to be two-faced, we learn to say something other than what we actually think. Some mentally ill people often have difficulty separating what they do from what the voices in their heads tell them to do, they do what the voices say, causing terrible problems.

Some people who are more balanced, apparently normal people, have learned that certain thoughts and feelings have to be suppressed, they present what is socially or politically correct even if they disagree, then when they are alone or with a group of likeminded people, they say what they really think. This is hypocrisy which has been described as satan's sin, a great sin. Hypocrisy means thinking one thing and saying something else, making others think we believe something when we do not, in order to achieve our ends.

Those who think this kind of hypocrisy is legitimate, because it is useful for their own purposes, believe this is a way to acquire what they want, things of value. In fact, it is not true, hypocrisy prevents something, it stops the growth of the individual. Even when it is

199

defined by a specific conflict, this hypocrisy supports duality, partnering the overriding sense of duality itself which needs to be eliminated. Most people fail to realize what hypocrisy does on this path of self-discovery, this path requiring a deep understanding of what goes on inside us. When we do what is right for appearance's sake, without any attachment to what is right, we have no love for it, we love only our desires.

The first thing we have to recognize is the truth of right and wrong; if we do not love what is right we have to learn what it is and learn to love it. To go on this path, to have what God has intended for us, to reach up to the truth, we have to overcome this hurdle—as long as there is no unity, no oneness within ourselves, there cannot be unity with others, among our fellow human beings and with God.

If we conceal aspects of ourselves from everyone else, sometimes we might be concealing these things from ourselves too. Why would we hide something from others that we expose to ourselves, that we keep hidden to relish at certain times in dark, hidden places? What is it that lets this happen, what is actually going on inside us to create dark corners, to be different privately from the way we are openly, how do we change that? We have to recognize that we do this before we can correct it. Only when we are so open that we look each other in the eye with nothing to hide, only then can we truly see ourselves.

As long as we have things to hide from other people they cannot see into us, and the same things which keep others from seeing into us blocks our ability to see ourselves accurately. What we think we are hiding from others is what we are hiding from ourselves. When we hide from ourselves, we are preventing the ability to see reality. The duality of hypocrisy contributes to this inability. When we know we do not feel what we are supposed to feel, we know we must change.

This is the work of the path, getting rid of that part of us which is not the truth, getting rid of that part of us which is not right. We need to straighten up, walk the right path and walk it easily, honestly, with good will, with positive intentions. This little bit of work, this little bit of understanding can take us a long way. Understand we have to be at peace within ourselves, and recognize that this peace allows us to expose who we really are to others, without fear, without shame, without agenda, then we turn to God without hypocrisy.

God is known in the Hebrew scriptures as 'I am that I am.' He is only One. To know this One we must be merged in One. Our hypocrisy must be eliminated, we cannot scheme or manipulate, we have to let go of thinking that way. There is a difference between being pure and being naïve; we have to understand the treachery of the world, see it and acknowledge it when we see it, but we cannot let it be part of us, we do not have to believe that for success in this world we must use such techniques. We need a group or community where people are not afraid, where they can be honest with each other, where they can let down their defenses and be open, show their true selves. Only when the true self is displayed can we begin to know it. As we begin to know the true self we begin to know the truth.

We have to be smaller individually, smaller as a community, so small we fit easily into each other. There is room for this if everything we have hidden inside ourselves filling us up, leaving no room for anyone else, is emptied. When we are without motive, when we do not scheme we become small, we are empty, there is room for Him. This is a key unlocking the doors of reality, one of the keys making Him available. When He is available we will be entirely empty, allowing Him to fill that space, but if we hold onto hypocrisy we are holding the devil's tail. As long as we hold onto evil, how can we possibly hold onto God? We have to make the choice, the choice is clear.

The great teachers and sages often talk about this. They tell us not to untie every little knot, but to pull the whole thing out by the roots and forget about it. If our thought patterns are too complicated, give them up. We are not complicated beings, not meant to be complicated, we are meant to be pure, we are meant to be clean, to be straight. The more we complicate things, the more difficult it is for us to be pure and clean and straight. This is not a complicated path, it is a straight path. It is called the straight path because it does not zigzag, it is direct. We have to be direct, we have to be people of the straight path, of straight action, we have to be people of love.

We should set the right intention encompassed by love. When love fills a room there is no space for anything else. Love numbs the lower self, it tames it; love lights a fire which the lower self backs away from, allowing grace to shine. It is a light, a fire, a cleansing, the cleansing we look for, the cleansing love which does away with duality. We no longer have to be divided, we are consistent in our speech, in our manner, in our love. Others can expect us to behave a certain way, to react a certain way, they do not have to fear how we will be today, how we will be this afternoon or the next time they see us.

We need to be comfortable enough with each other to know we are a comfort for each other. This starts in our home, we need to be a comfort for each other at home, we need to know when we turn to our spouse, that person is a rock for us, we need to be a rock for each other. The ability to comfort moves out from our family to our circle of friends. The circle of true friends is the circle of those who are a comfort for each other, a sanctuary for each other. We become the place we can live within in safety, in love, in protection. Small, easy things change our life, change our attitudes, change who we are, our perspective, the way we act and feel in our daily life. If we can take ourselves to that level of comfort our center is stronger.

We know what a locked box is, the sort of box we should put our hypocrisy in; however, with all the problems of the world we go searching for the key to open it up again because we think we need it. We should reach a point where we no longer need it, reach a point where we do not have to join all the barking dogs, we can walk away and let the dogs bark. Walking away from a group of barking dogs, stepping away from the fray is difficult, letting other people argue, letting them offer their opinions without being involved, without telling them how they are right and how they are wrong is difficult.

We have stories about wise people who do not talk, do not

respond. There is a story about a group who had come to pray at a roadside mosque. While they were sitting after prayers another man came to pray who prayed facing the wrong direction, but no one said anything. When they stood to pray at the next time of prayer, facing the right direction, he understood his mistake and joined them. This was done without a word, without a reprimand, it was done through action, it was done by doing what is right. We must incorporate our intention in our action; actions are stronger than words. We must incorporate our intention in our resonance; our resonance is stronger than words. We can feel each other, know where we are, know where each of us is. We should know we are comfortable with each other, feel we are comfortable with each other, easy with each other. We should know that love exists, we should understand the sanctuary of our family and spread that understanding, that love, one person at a time. It does not have to be done with words at first, people recognize when something special is happening, they ask why, then we can talk about it because they have recognized there is something else.

Until people recognize something else exists and have a taste for it, it is difficult to bring them to this path, it could even be dangerous. Nevertheless, we should know that bringing others along is part of what He has given us to do, and once we know it is our responsibility, it will happen. We can help just by being the way we are. It is a great blessing to have this in our life, it is a gift He has granted to give us access to Him. To understand this and create praise for Him is the reason the prophets were sent, the reason the wise, holy beings and His friends were sent. How do we become His friend? We become His friend by being a friend of His friend, by respecting His friends, listening to His friends, listening to those who have listened to Him.

May we begin to understand ourselves, study ourselves and be one within ourselves. May the words which come from our mouth be straight, clean and pure, without motive, filled with love. May the blessings that come from this love bathe us in His love.

*God did have a reason
to create man.*

The Creation of Adam

The creation of Adam, the first man, is a great mystery, and we are all related to this mystery in a very significant way. To understand who we are, we have to understand who Adam is, what his creation means because we are a re-creation of that original creation. To know ourselves we can start with these questions, why was this species called man created, why did God create Adam?

We have been told by the scriptures that God created the world and other beings before He created man. When God told the angels that He was going to create a being who would be greater than they were, with a capacity to know Him greater than their own, a certain angel objected. This angel was sure this being would not be obedient, he would not do what God said, he would kill other creatures and argue with God. What the angel could not understand, and what we find difficult to understand, is a state higher than our own. The disobedient angel could not understand God's reasons for creating man because the angel did not know what God knew. In just the same way, we often assume things we cannot understand, we are limited by what we know, limited by our own state.

God did have a reason to create man. The rest of creation had been brought into existence as things which He produced from Himself yet not from His essence. He wanted to create something that came from His essence. The Old Testament says that God created man in His own image although we are told that God has no image, we are told that God is incomparable, we are told not to create pictures or representations of Him, nevertheless, He created man in His own image. Why would God want to create something in His own image, why would He want to create something unto Himself?

Before the beginningless beginning, God knew Himself through Himself, there was nothing else, there was only God. In His vastness He understood His own being, yet we can only understand other things by looking at them. To see ourselves we need a mirror, but think about looking at a mirror without any backing while still being able to see ourselves, to know ourselves. God knew Himself in a way we cannot understand, He knew Himself by looking within Himself, there was no external reflection or image. He knew Himself from within Himself, but He wanted to know Himself from without as well, He wanted to know Himself as a reflection of Himself.

God decided to create a vice-regent in this world, a king for the world under His dominion. He wanted to make something in this world which included everything within itself, in the way that everything was included within Himself. Of course this creation is not God, we cannot make that mistake, but this creation is the closest thing to God in the created universe. This thing He created He called Adam, the first man who was given dominion over the whole world. It is said that God created the world with two hands, everything else with one hand, but when He created man He also blew His breath into him, something which separates us from the rest of creation.

We walk around with God's breath within us, that breath which is the soul exists within us. As a symbol of His breath within us we are sustained by breath, our breath never stops, if it stops we stop. Just as our breath sustains us, God sustains the world, He continues to sustain the world.

Interestingly enough, when Adam was given dominion over everything he was unhappy even though he controlled the world, all the creatures, everything in the world. He had a relationship with God which was a response to something higher than himself, in that sense a limited relationship, and he asked God for a companion he could have a relationship with on his own level, as a way to know himself.

As God wanted to create a being who would know Him, understand Him and reflect Him so that His glory would be more evident, Adam wanted the same thing. The response to his request was a companion, Eve. Much later on, the prophet Muhammad would tell us that half our path lies in marriage, we come to know ourselves through marriage. How do we come to know God? By knowing ourselves. This means the most important relationship we have in our worldly life is our marriage, and the second most important relationship in this world is with the rest of humanity. God put what he gave Adam in all of us, we have an opportunity to recognize it in everyone. Some of us recognize God in ourselves yet we fail to see God in everyone else, rather like the angel who objected to the creation of Adam.

Satan complained that God would create a being unlike Him, separate from Him, a creature who would do things with appalling consequences for His creation. This is the kind of thing some of us now say about other people. When we do, what are we like, what are we imitating and why? We say this because we do not recognize what satan and his followers refused to recognize in man. We refuse to bow to others while we bow to ourselves, we will not give that respect to others

When we do not recognize God in ourselves, we are looking at our base desires, the animal aspect of our nature, yet we are different from the animals on this planet. If we look upon others as animals it means we have seen only the animal in ourselves. If we see others as higher beings close to God, if we see the soul, the breath of God in other beings we can understand that in ourselves. If we cannot see it in others we cannot see it in ourselves.

The ability to act correctly is such an important part of our life. How can we trust God if we do not trust what He has placed in others? How can we be worthy of trust? Either we are worthy of it or we are not. Our proving ground for trustworthiness lies in our relations with the world, beginning with the family, the way we act within the family, expanding then to our relations with teachers, with friends and acquaintances.

If we say something, how important is our word, is it meaningful, are we conscious of what comes out of our mouth, are we conscious of the way we act? Do we understand what is right, is this understanding a part of our life? God created us as His vice-regent, His trustee for this domain, and that implies His trust in us. We need to acquire a level of trust by earning the trust of those around us; we trust their hearts and they trust ours.

We need to recognize our sameness, this immense glory where the unity of God exists. As we move away from this sameness we step into separation, the realm of separation from God. If we resist affection from our companions we resist affection for God, if we resist associating with our friends and family we resist associating with God. If we try to assert superiority over them we are trying to be superior to God, if we try to be the authority instead of letting them have their say we are trying to have authority over God.

We are all made from the same cloth and woven on the same loom, we came from one Creator. Anyone who says your God is different from my God has a god who is just an idol. Either we believe there is one God or we do not, if we believe it then He is everyone's God. We need to know our place in creation because the story of Adam is our story. Until we learn that every story is our story we cannot know ourselves. There is only one story, His story, the one we have to include in our existence.

We should learn the complete history of His story, the reason for the things He created. We should go to the realm of wisdom which lies beyond intellect. Wisdom cannot be explained by science, it can only be learned from those who live in that realm, who are in touch with divine knowledge, true knowledge which they have received from others who had that wisdom. Sometimes it appears that this knowledge has been lost to the world, that it cannot be recovered, but it is not lost, it is merely not searched for. We have to search, we have to make that effort.

The world is a powerful place, everything God produced, everything He created has a certain kind of power or force, powers which have magnetic properties, hypnotic properties which fascinate us. We have a choice to make, we can be fascinated or we can move towards God. The world can point us to God or to the things of the world. It depends on the direction we choose, we can pursue the things of the world or understand that these things point to God.

A sanctified being once said the world is God's translator. Either we use the world to translate God for us, or we try to find the meaning of the world. If we try to find the meaning of the world it's like peeling an onion, nothing is there at the end. If we are not looking for God there is nothing to find, He is the only thing there is to find. When we go in search of the wrong thing we are never satisfied. One main ingredient on this path is love, this is the path of love. We cannot form the right relationship with others, unless we care for others, unless we care for them we cannot have the respect for them necessary to establish appropriate respect for ourselves, appropriate respect for God. May we understand the nature of creation and proceed on that path to Him, the path He created for us.

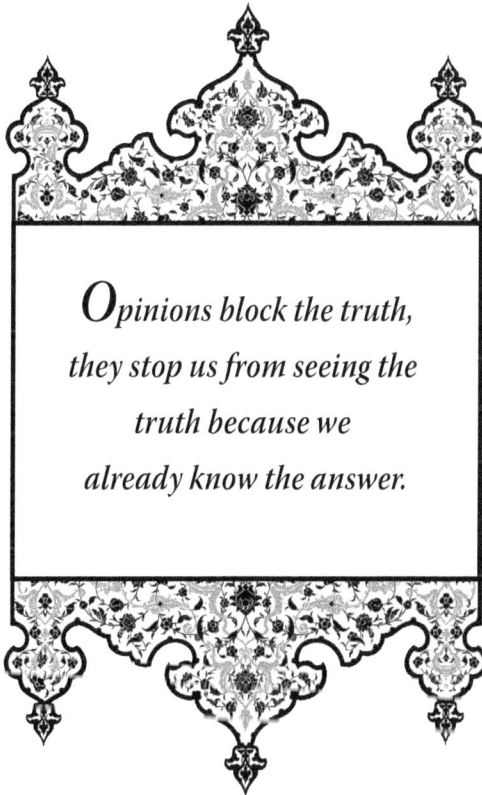

*Opinions block the truth,
they stop us from seeing the
truth because we
already know the answer.*

Examining the Self

The koala lives among eucalyptus trees where the leaves are its food, leaves which are poisonous to most other species but nourishment to the koala. Since these leaves are not a great source of nourishment they have to keep eating all day to get enough. It is a small creature which has found a place to live where nothing attacks it, where it is left in peace to eat as much as it wants. People live near the North Pole, a place most of us think would be impossible to live near, yet a small society flourishes there. Polar bears live on the ice, the cold which is difficult for many of us is life for the polar bear. The different scenarios of sustenance we cannot understand or tolerate do not mean others are not benefiting from them, even being kept alive by them. Certain things we discard or run from are keeping others alive. This should help us reconsider how we look at things, how irrelevant our conclusions can be when we judge things by our own requirements.

We have different aspects of the self, some parts antithetic to other parts, certain parts of us cannot exist while other parts are in control. How we behave depends on our disposition at a given moment, but the range of variations is remarkable. Some who drift to extremes beyond their ability to control are described as bipolar, they behave in such seriously opposite ways from time to time they cannot function adequately. If we met such a person in his manic state and formed an opinion based on that, and someone else met this person in his depressed state and formed an opinion based on that, the two of us would seem to be talking about two different people. We all have these changes to a certain extent, when some aspects prevail others recede so far into the background they more or less cease to exist. If we do not control our energies, control our state, what comes up determines what someone else sees. We might develop quite different relationships with different people—mutual acquaintances could think they are not talking about the same individual, even without any bipolar extremes.

We need to know who we are to make sense of who we are, but how do we figure this out when we have so many different inner individuals to deal with? Are we the happy person or the sad person, are we energetic or the person who cannot get out of bed, are we capable or unable to do anything, are we brilliant or ignorant, are we passive or active? Since we are all of them at one time or another, how do we negotiate the differences, how do we determine which one we are?

Children often go through a phase known as the terrible twos, a time when they are out of control, totally self-centered, wanting everything. Without the language to express their needs they cry until someone understands what they want. Slowly we learn to communicate, how to make what we want known, a process called socialization, learning to be civilized, learning appropriate conduct. Different cultures and traditions have different names for this, different rules specifying how to act. Parts of us do not know how to act, aspects of the self are overwhelmed by desire, insisting on having their own way. This is our lower self, that part of us which insists on being in control, insists on fulfilling desire without considering the circumstances, the consequences. There is a traditional story about the prophet Muhammad which reveals something about this. It seems the prophet was asked if he had any base desires. His answer was yes, he did have, but he had made them all believers, he had taught them all to adhere scrupulously to what is appropriate. They had been taught proper conduct, they had been trained.

We have all seen dogs bark and jump even though they are on

a leash, making the owner exert a great effort to keep them from attacking. Other dogs listen to their master's commands and do what they are supposed to do. We each have different dogs within whose behavior depends on how we treat them, some are like the dogs in the street who lunge at whatever they see, others walk quietly along. Those lunging dogs cannot be controlled, they do not listen to our commands because we have not trained them as we became adults. Why haven't we done that? This is a hard question implying we have not done something we ought to have done. What is missing in us, why didn't we train the dog? As we walk down the street with our dog jumping at people, we enjoy seeing them jump, we enjoy their fright. Forget about the dog on a leash, what about the satisfaction we take from the responses to the dogs inside us, what about the things we allow our inner dogs to do? Do we enjoy this, do we think we enjoy this? Do we fail to train them because we find satisfaction in their misconduct? In other words, we like that, we do not want to change it. There are those who preach if it feels good, it is acceptable. Who defines what feels good for us, what defines how far we go before we put on the brakes, before we put the dog on some kind of leash?

Animal trainers know they cannot tame a wild animal in a few seconds, minutes, hours or days, it is a continuing process. This is the sort of taming we have to become adept at. We have seen television shows with someone who trains dogs by whispering to them, commanding them to behave in ways their owners cannot. We have also seen shows with a nanny who trains children in households where the parents have no ability to control their children. At the end of the training an out of control child or animal is usually under control, they have been taught new habits which make them easier to deal with. When we look at the behavior of abusive husbands for example, we see that after episodes of abuse some keep apologizing for what they have done, yet they return to being abusive, and they also return to apologizing. Some alcoholics often become despondent after they drink, but they do go back to drinking. This is a failure to recognize and control our dogs, to be aware of our habits, the inner conditioning which is out of control.

How do we proceed to bring about control, which of all the diverging worldly opinions do we choose? Suppose we want to do something about sexual desire, suppose we are looking for guides to regulate sexual desire. If we study certain magazines and follow their advice we will behave a certain way, but if we take our advice from scriptures we will behave differently, we will develop different solutions. This means the first thing we need to do is decide on a teacher, even if we are self-taught we still need guidebooks to point us in the right direction. The choice is ours, we decide which way to go. In this country we are quite free to do almost anything we want, in some countries we have to hide things, but here there are instruction manuals to take us any way we want to go.

Some of us meet as a group because we have decided to follow a specific way, a specific set of principles, the way instituted by the prophets of God, their instructions on appropriate conduct. The next step is learning what these instructions are, incorporating them, training different aspects of the self to follow them. There is an outer and inner side to these instructions, we can learn how to act outwardly without knowing the corresponding inner state, but we cannot behave inappropriately on the outside and believe we are being appropriate.

Actions can be controlled two ways, by force or by understanding the reality of who we are. When we want babies to behave a certain way, first we show them how to do something, then they begin to understand. Before we truly understand we need to learn how to act correctly, how to stop what is incorrect. We start with simple things, we do not steal. We might not know why we do not, we just know that we do not, knowing we do not steal is sufficient, we need to know nothing more than that. Other things are more subtle, the more subtle they are the more we have to be in a state of being which understands. Now what does this state mean? It means the ability to displace the will and needs of our lower self with the will we can develop through a study of all the holy scriptures, what we learn from the prophets, from the resonance of reality, the truth of God's resonance in this world. Essentially, this true state of being means the surrender of the self which allows that One to come through us, to blow through us, instructing us, teaching us to act appropriately.

This is difficult when we have opinions about everything, ideas about everything. Opinions block the truth, they stop us from seeing the truth because we already know the answer. Once when my wife and I were walking past a church we heard gospel singing in a style we found intriguing. We walked inside where they seated us courteously to listen. There was so much resonance in that church. When the singing finished the pastor announced they had a guest, pointing to me, then asked if I would like to say anything. As a stranger I felt reluctant to say much, but they had a sign on their wall reminding us that in diversity we could find our strength. I repeated what the sign said, saying quietly if we could follow this truth we would go much further in wonderful ways, and sat down.

I had a great personal moment in that church, in touch with reality. If my preconceptions had stopped me from going there I would have missed it. Just as we find it hard to believe that people live at the North Pole, that koalas live on eucalyptus, we find it hard to believe that people take their nourishment in different ways. We recognize how much work we still have to do on those immature, imperfect places within ourselves, why should we judge the process going on somewhere else, why should we judge someone else's nourishment?

A wise man watching an animal eat an insect said if the animal truly understood what was inside the insect he would not eat it. If we truly understood what is inside each other, understood the process everyone must undergo, we would leave each other in peace and be supportive, we need to be as supportive with each other as we are with ourselves, as supportive with ourselves as we are with each other. Some find it easy to be generous to others but not to themselves, others find it easy to be generous to themselves but not to others. This is a two-way street.

In Rūmī's Mathnawī, someone asks 'Umar ibnul-Khattāb why God placed the soul in man causing all this suffering. 'Umar replies by asking why there is a presumption of suffering, the question postulates a wrong answer when creation itself exists in a way beyond the understanding of the person who asked. 'Umar tells him he has placed limits on himself which stop God's grace, he should be quiet about things he does not understand, stop asking questions with sour answers already planted in the question. We need to recognize when we are being sour while pretending to be sweet, being sour while pretending to understand. The devious nature of intellect and ego is beyond imagination, the forces of darkness and illusion keep tricking us with negative attitudes presenting them as truth. We have to turn away from the negativity of darkness and be firm in belief, positive, a helping hand in this world.

The prophets came to this world as a mercy from God. Are we part of that mercy? We should act to become part of that mercy, then our own inner problems will be addressed, then we can reach out to help everything all around us. May we do this work which takes us on the straight, true path to God, reflecting His light.

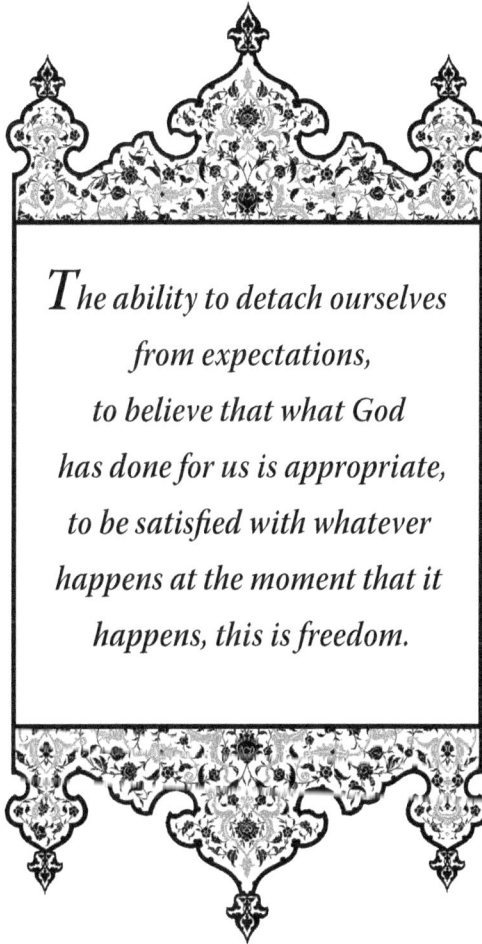

*The ability to detach ourselves
from expectations,
to believe that what God
has done for us is appropriate,
to be satisfied with whatever
happens at the moment that it
happens, this is freedom.*

Freedom

Freedom, a word often used in politics, means many different things. Right now there is much in the news about adequate social security which gives older people economic freedom. We see freedom in different ways: there are guarantees of certain freedoms in our Constitution, freedom of assemblage, freedom of religion, freedom of speech. They mean we have the legal right to do certain things without prosecution, without the involvement of government institutions. In our world freedom means, in part, the ability to carry on without interference from government institutions.

In other parts of the world, the way people act and the things they do and say are subject to what the government dictates. In the founding of America there was an attempt to establish a government less involved with what we do individually, less interested. In many places the government has an interest in what the people do because they fear them. Freedom on an individual basis however, is something quite different from our relationship with a government. Freedom is our ability to be free of anxiety, free enough of the torments of existence to let us understand where this freedom can be found, where we can be free to be at peace, free to understand the kind of freedom we are talking about.

The world might tell us we are free when we have more power than the next person, that we are free if we can overpower others, we are free when we are beyond their influence. The world tells us freedom means we have enough money to do what we want, yet if we look at powerful men, if we look at rulers and observe their burdens, we wonder about their freedom. If we study powerful men and their problems, if we study wealthy men and see what they do to maintain that wealth, we wonder what freedom they have.

What we learn from those examples is that people are attached to maintaining things as they are, to holding onto what they think they have, maintaining the status quo. For these people this means they are in control, freedom for them means being in control. However, if we try to control the recurring chaos of the world in a specific way, we are certain to be tossed around. Our freedom is subject to things not necessarily under our control, not subject to the pressure we apply for the results we are attached to. If we are attached to specific results, if we are attached to a certain order of things, our freedom is troubled as we keep trying to change things, to make us finally feel free. Chasing that freedom, that peace, is our constant effort.

This is the consequence of a worldly definition, while the definition of freedom on the path means being a servant to our Lord, servanthood to the Master, freedom lies in our servanthood. The ability to detach ourselves from expectations, to believe that what God has done for us is appropriate, to be satisfied with whatever happens at the moment that it happens, this is freedom. If we can bring ourselves to that state there is freedom. As long as we push, as long as we pull, as long as we want and need, there is no freedom.

Some teaching stories try to explain this in a certain way. These stories are often about kings trying to find freedom in the context of a kingdom they have to give up. Other stories may be about beggars who have so little, a penny or a loincloth which they have to give up. The beggar who has so little and the king who has so much both have to give up the same thing, everything they have. There is equality in God's justice, everyone is treated the same way. God wants the same thing from everyone, He wants everything, the more we accumulate, the more important this accumulation seems to us.

Here is an illustration. There was once a poor man who used to work chopping wood. At the end of each day he was paid five rupees which he used to buy fruit to share with his friends. They would play soccer, eat the fruit, then the man would go to bed, tired from work and play. The next day he chopped wood again, earned his five rupees and repeated the same thing.

Now a rich man lived in a big house on a hill overlooking the hut where the poor man lived, and he used to watch the woodchopper, observing the freedom of the poor man's life, his fearlessness. The rich man who lived on the hill had become a miser over the years, preserving and hanging onto what he had. Frustrated by what he kept seeing down below, he went to a wise man, "You know, I have a great deal but I can't spend a penny on fruit, yet this man who chops wood spends everything he has. I don't understand."

The wise man said, "Fill a bag with ninety-nine rupees and throw it into his hut when the woodchopper is out. Watch to see what happens."

He did this, and when the woodchopper came back that evening he found the bag, then he began to count one, two, three, four, five, six rupees, he'd never seen so much. Six rupees altogether were the most he had ever seen at one time in his life. He went on counting, seven, eight, until he had finally counted the ninety-nine. Standing at the entrance to his little hut he said, "O God, thank you for the gift of ninety-nine rupees You have given me. If only You could give me one more I would have a hundred."

The next day when he went to chop wood things were different, now he needed to save some money to get the hundred he wanted, but as soon as he had that much he thought, "With a little effort I would have two hundred." The poor man could no longer buy fruit, and he no longer had the companionship of the friends who were even poorer than he was. Without the fruit they just stopped coming around. Slowly his life began to change, he became reclusive, a smaller version of the rich man on the hill who continued to watch with interest.

Either we are drawn closer to the world in our life, collecting the things of the world, or we spend our time getting rid of the world. Either we try to become a master of the world, or a servant to the Creator of the world. Our freedom lies in servanthood, our freedom is the ability to understand the relationship between man and God, understand our place in that relationship as a servant. The ability to become small is the ability to be free. The world tells us we need more, there is no growth in giving things away, growth means saving it all up, accumulation, swallowing the whole world if we can, then we are most important.

The opposite is true. Freedom comes when our attachments are finished, when our relationship with the world becomes less important and the relationship with God becomes more important. When we begin to lose our sense of self, we become greater, greater in the sense that we are part of something which is greater. Things of the world and interaction with the world separate us from this greater thing. The more we interact in an accumulating way, motivated by the self, the more we leave our servanthood behind. We can be a king or we can be a servant, it is possible to be either. The freedom we have in this country means we can be the king of our own castle, we no longer have to be a servant to other men, we no longer have to be a slave to other men. Yet we do have to take on a new understanding of servanthood, not to other men but to God.

Submission in prayer is an exalted position. Understand the greatness of living in the world of inner contemplation and satisfaction, removed from the push and pull of the things all around us. We withdraw from those externals, although not like a recluse afraid of interaction with others. There is an inner path which lets us be in the world but not of it, we walk with God in the world yet separate from it. This is the path we are studying; we do not leave the world, we do not become hermits, we tell the world we believe in it but we do not, we believe in God. Understand this state of belief with the trust which separates us from all the pulls of the world, pulls which can be difficult if we are lost in desire, if we want rewards for the good things we do, or if we fear punishment for whatever is inappropriate.

In the place of desire, of reward and punishment, we live in a world of praise and blame, a world of opposites where everything has two sides. When we keep searching for the easy way, simultaneously we fear the difficult way, we fear something which looks hard. We should avoid attachments, and avoid this way of thinking. When we are torn by different ways to do something, it is important to stand back from the struggle of conflicting thoughts— once we abandon the struggle the right way might become apparent. As long as the struggling sides within us compete, the competition leads to chaos, like an external fight. Part of us insists on one way and another part insists on some other way, a civil war, a war which does no good for a country or a person.

The fight inside ourselves, do this, don't do this, do that, don't do that, this is the confusion and chaos we are subject to. It would be laughable if it were not such torture. The way out of this civil war is to let go of the attachment to what is perceived as a satisfying result. As long as we are looking for satisfaction out there in the world this turmoil goes on, but when we relieve ourselves of those attachments the turmoil stops. To reach the place of servanthood we need to understand what a servant does: a servant serves the Master for the sake of the Master. A servant does not accumulate things for himself, he does not expect anything for himself, his satisfaction lies in appropriate duty, in appropriate reaction to the Master, to the King. We have to put ourselves in that place, be dutiful, be able to do our duty on behalf of the King, in an unselfish way. We have to do our duty to the King, not because of what we receive, because of the truth.

The great saint Rābi'ah said she wanted God, she did not want heaven and she was not afraid of hell. She was not interested in reward or punishment, she was there for her Master, for the joy of her Master, not because of what would or would not happen to her. We should understand that being engaged with the world, when we seek reward and avoid punishment when we need praise and fear criticism, all this traps us. When we are affected by the things which trap us, which do not let us be free, we are trapped and attached inwardly and outwardly to things implanted when we were young. We were told if we are good this happens, if we are bad that happens. We should be relieved of these thoughts, cleared of mental influences, cleared of the inner animals who all clamor for attention, for what they want.

There is a zoo of different intentions inside us. Learn how to cleanse them, how to tame the animals, keep them under control, on a leash. The prophet Muhammad was once asked, "Don't you have a whole menagerie inside you like the rest of us, don't you have the base desires we have?"

He answered, "Yes, but I've trained mine to be believers."

We have to train our desires to be believers, train every inner thing into submission, tame them. A cow gives itself to its master without complaint, with great compliance. This does not mean we should be cows, God did not create us as cows, He created us with free will. We need to struggle into active submission, be active servants with a purpose, be content in servanthood, then freedom is available, peace is available, the real treasure of creation is available.

It has been said that the treasure lies hidden in the ruins, and those who live in servanthood are the ruins. They might appear to be abandoned, but if we look closely we can see that God lives in them, He lives in certain abandoned beings who seem so small, so hidden away we cannot find them. We should hide like that, apparently ruined outwardly but lit with the radiant light of truth within. This is the inner treasure of God's grace, the truth which comes with the understanding that part of us is from Him. When we are in touch with that part of ourselves, that part submits. Who submits to whom? This is our path, the path we need to understand. Know what pulls us from this path and what pulls us towards it. May God make it easy to be pulled to Him.

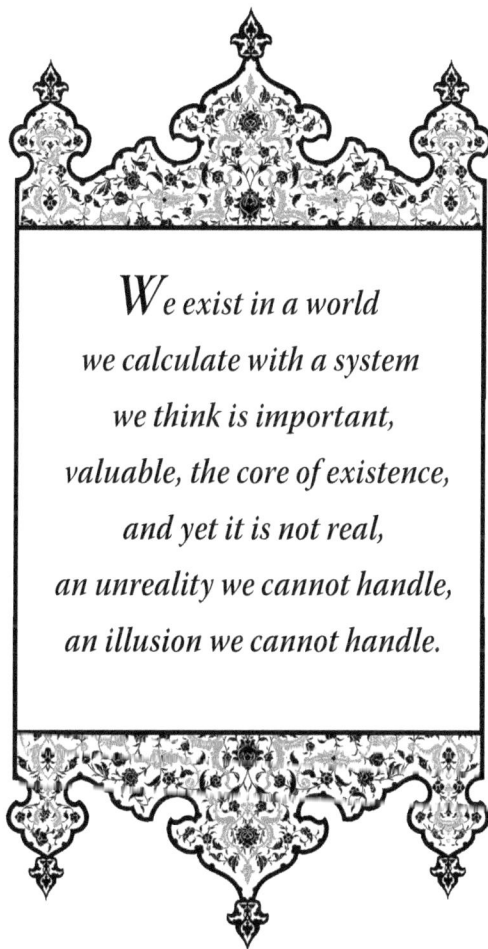

*We exist in a world
we calculate with a system
we think is important,
valuable, the core of existence,
and yet it is not real,
an unreality we cannot handle,
an illusion we cannot handle.*

Understanding Illusion

If you speak to an Eskimo about the world, his description is quite different from the Zulu's in South Africa. Both versions of the world find the other incomprehensible, each might think the other is make-believe, an illusion or a lie. From the Eskimo perspective the Zulu world is an illusion, a lie, and from the Zulu perspective the Eskimo world is an illusion, a lie. Both have developed language and culture which reflect the world they live in, which make it possible to communicate within the parameters of their world. If we take either from his world and put him in the other, his culture and language would have to change dramatically, the habits of his life would have to change, everything would have to be turned upside down.

We all come from a certain culture, we all have certain habits, we have all learned how to get along in the circumstances we accept. If someone told us we were living a lie, most of us would think that was wrong. Before we could believe that something exists besides what we know through touch, smell, sight, hearing and taste, we would require solid proof because we believe in these things, this is the way we understand the world.

When someone tells us all this is a lie, that none of what we see and hear is true, we are incredulous, angry, someone is misrepresenting the way we live, throwing our socioeconomic existence into turmoil. Someone who talks this way is dangerous, if people no longer believe in our system it falls apart. When our life is attached to a system, when it is dependent on a system, especially if we are in power, a religious leader, a political leader, we might react violently to someone describing the system as a lie.

The whole world suffers from this to a certain extent. The Sanskrit root of the word illusion means to measure. One thing we use in our daily life is mathematics, one plus one equals two, we have learned how to count, and by counting we can do many useful things in the gross world of things we live in. We know if three people are coming to dinner we need three plates, useful information. Historically, there was a time when counting was about as much as could be done in mathematics, but it advanced beyond mere counting. An ancient Greek geometry text has precise mathematical calculations. They called the outside of a circle the circumference, a line dividing it through the center the diameter, half the diameter they called the radius. They found that if they divided the radius into the circumference they got a ratio, a consistent ratio for every radius in every circle. They called this pi, discovering that with the radius of a circle they could calculate the circumference of any circle using this ratio.

As algebra was developed we could calculate an unknown quantity from other known quantities. In school we are taught simple mathematics to solve a problem: if a train travels at sixty miles an hour, how far will it go in two hours? Newtonian physics came later. Physics determined ways of identifying things in the world around us, explaining how things work. Later, Einstein changed this understanding with relativity. If things move at a certain speed, things are altered, they change. The things we have been counting and the way we have counted do not accommodate this change.

When science became more sophisticated with the capacity to study smaller and smaller particles, it entered the subatomic world and found that the laws of geometry and Newtonian physics, which had been taken as a description of reality, no longer held together. Something else was happening in the smaller and smaller subatomic world, they could no longer predict what would happen with the tools they had used for measuring, there were influences beyond their ability to measure, influences they could not explain, know where they came from or what they were. Everything science had measured in the past had mass. If we hit something we hurt our hand, but suddenly there were things which had no apparent mass whose influence could be detected.

Now everything we see, hear, taste, touch and calculate makes no sense in the subatomic world we also belong to. What holds us together is what we expect when we look with our eyes, touch with our hands or smell with our nose. This outer illusion has been explained in many ways, but we are not to believe what we see with the outer eye, we are to see with the inner eye; we are not to believe what we hear with the outer ear, we are to hear with the inner ear; we are not to believe what we smell with the outer nostrils, we are to detect smell with the inner nostril; we are to taste with the inner tongue, use the inner sense apparatus.

We exist in a world we calculate with a system we think is important, valuable, the core of existence, and yet it is not real, an unreality we cannot handle, an illusion we cannot handle. We cannot float in a space we do not understand, do not believe in because we have been taught to think of things as concrete in nature. Now our world is falling apart, we need something to hold it together, we need it to make sense. We are like the Zulu who is told the world is all ice and snow, he thinks we are mad or deluded. If we say our world, including ourselves, is made up of particles without mass, some might say we are also mad or deluded.

God is atomless, without mass, without form. He is not created, He is not part of what we think we see, He is something else. Now go to the subatomic world where we find particles of influence which have no mass, particles science has named that we will rename. Let us call one compassion, let us call another mercy, another patience, another gratitude, another forgiveness, another forbearance. These are influences that predict and control, influences without mass and without form which exist within each of us. They exist as who and what we are, yet we do not see what cannot be seen and we do not believe it because we believe in what we see, what society calls normal. Someone who lives in the Arctic wilderness may think the world is white, covered in snow, someone who lives in a remote rain forest may think the world is green and wet. What do we believe, what can we believe? How important is it to understand the world we live in, can we exist knowing that we do not know very much? Can we exist in the understanding that we live in His grace, we rely on His mercy and His compassion for our existence, that we have nothing to do with it?

We have been told that only God can know God, that God is our only true friend, He is compassionate, He is merciful, He is just, patient and tolerant. Who are we? If we are also made of all these things, are we part of God or have we created something else we call ourselves? If God is the totality, everything which exists, is it possible to say we are not Godly? Is it possible to say I am right and you are wrong, is it possible to say that I am appropriate, you are not? Is it possible to say my color is right but yours is not, my position is higher than yours, my birth is higher than yours?

If we are all made of that essence which is His, is your essence different from His? Do we understand this or do we create idols to worship because we cannot separate ourselves from our senses, from our eyes, our nose, our ears, our taste, our sense of smell? We need something to hold onto, we cannot live in the open space of reality. We cannot enter the world of the soul with the body we live in, and so we do not believe we can go there at all. What is the core of our belief, who are we, how do we think? Do we realize if we are to become like God we have to become those subatomic influences without form, without shape and without mass? We must become compassion, we must become mercy, we must become tolerance, kindness and justice. As we become all this the gross and material which can be measured are much less important, and now we begin to vibrate with reality.

Suddenly we understand illusion. If we are not just we cannot understand illusion, if we are not merciful we cannot understand illusion, if we are angry we cannot understand illusion. If we are resentful we cannot understand illusion because we are the illusion we label reality. We have to grasp this understanding with subtlety or else our path is hopelessly tied to illusion, dependent on illusion. If we are filled with ego and self-importance we have to be important, our religion has to be important. This is the world of praise and blame. Without praise and blame we cannot make comparisons, without comparisons we cannot have higher and lower, we cannot have that sense of differences which illusion depends on. Illusion exists to maintain the appearance of differences; as long as we live in a place which depends on differences we cannot leave illusion, they very thing we have to do. To know reality we have to leave illusion, to leave illusion we have to leave the illusory version of our existence, and this is not easy. Concrete can only be altered by shattering it, but steel can be melted down and reformed.

We cannot become part of reality unless we change, we cannot live in the truth unless we alter ourselves, change from the gross to the subtle, to the nonexistent. We must be nonexistent in the world of illusion, and when we grasp this point we can be a friend to others as our truth befriends theirs. God is our friend, God in us becomes a friend to God in them. Then there is real love in the world because His love recognizes His love in the other; the other and the self are one, rooted in reality, love is without mass, without form, atomless, yet reality.

It is not easy to sustain this way of thinking because our nature is dualistic, a painful fact. If we cannot sustain this paradox we cannot live in reality. Even if it is painful, that duality is not real. My faith must be strong enough so that every illusory proof put before me will not change my belief. The great holy beings were sent to this world to manifest our atomless creation. These pure qualities without form are holy. Before we can enter that holy state we have to be in the transcendent purity which protects us from all the invasive forces of illusion. This means we have to engage certain new ways, wrap ourselves in these new ways, walk that way, hide our eyes from certain things, hide our ears from certain things, learn not to say certain things. We have to watch our tongue, watch our life, be careful with it.

We have a choice to make, we can do one of two things, surrender to the truth or accumulate those forces inside us which deny the truth, which keep out the truth and establish a permanent connection to illusion. We do this once we assign reality to the world of mass, once we enter the world of comparisons, the world of praise and blame. As we do this we drift further away from the truth; as we move further away from the world of mass we move towards truth; as we move towards His qualities we come closer to truth; as we violate those qualities we drift away from truth. We never harm God with anything we do, we only harm ourselves. People devise many ways to enter illusion, including the thought they are protecting truth. Truth does not need protection, it exists, it has always existed, it will always exist. Truth protects us.

Some of the tools we use in the world are useful if they are focused on God—if we yearn for God, this yearning can be cured. Every other desire takes us nowhere, yet if we long for God this is a longing with a cure. Use what we have been taught, but use it pointed towards the truth. We pray that the steps we take are appropriate, that our yearning is appropriate and that our actions are appropriate. We pray that God accepts these prayers and takes us towards Him.

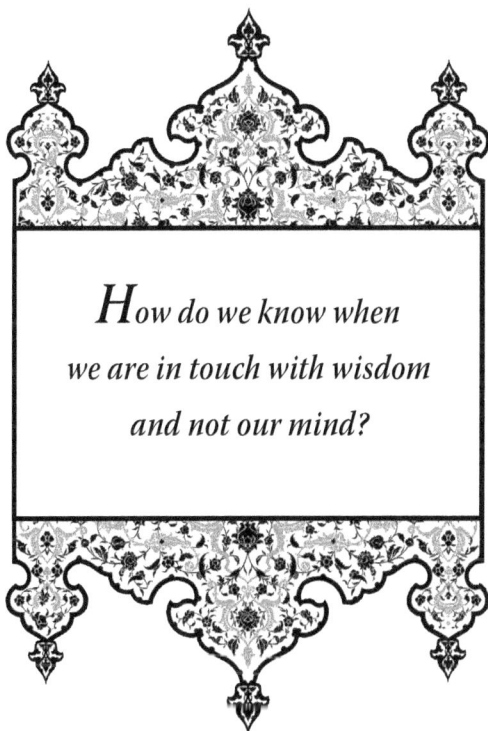

How do we know when
we are in touch with wisdom
and not our mind?

Levels of Understanding

People in the world seem to be filled with anxiety about the future, anxiety about what will happen next—just consider how many prescriptions for antidepressants are written every day. We should ask ourselves if we have been caught in that web of worry and fret, that web of anxiety, then try to understand what worry really is. We are told that worry means feeling future pain now, as if we can predict the future, as if we know what is going to happen, conclude the worst and feel that pain now. This is common, a self-created problem, we create our dilemma and suffer from its creation.

All this originates in the mind's attempt to control us, to keep us in a vulnerable state which prevents us from finding our true self, from understanding our birthright, knowing what is truly available. This means the forces of illusion have won their battle, all they have to do is keep us fretting, keep us worrying and uncomfortable, in a state of anxiety. These states are veils separating us from reality, veils we often create for ourselves, hiding behind those very attachments we should break.

We have followed patterns of behavior since we were young, patterns which are difficult to break. It is important to find some repeated action to dislodge these patterns, important to discover new pattern breaking habits. We recognize our bad habits, now we should acquire good habits, commit ourselves to these good habits in place of the bad ones which have occupied our life. The best habit is the elimination of these veils with an inner insistence that they do not exist, that reality alone exists which has nothing to do with veils. We have to empty ourselves, literally empty ourselves. When we practice the remembrance of God in conjunction with the breath, understand the first part of this is an emptying. Physiologically, we have to empty ourselves through our breath, it must be breathing with the realization we are ridding ourselves of illusions, an active, engaged effort. This requires the intention to ask for God's help because we cannot do it by ourselves. We combine our intention with our breath and breathe out the world of illusion through our left nostril, then we inhale through our right nostril, affirming the reality of God alone.[1]

How do we make our intention firm, how do we rid ourselves of anxiety? One way is understanding how our mind works, not giving it credence, an important step in relief from a never ending assault. What happens when we resolve one difficulty or drama, the mind presents us with another, then if we resolve that, another comes, it does not stop. It is important to know it will not stop. How do we deal with an inner drama which is not going to stop? We deal with it by recognizing the nature of the dilemma, recognizing and acknowledging our interaction with it. We have all known people we do not pay attention to, people who tell us things we know to be unreliable. Our mind is like that, not a reliable source of information on how to live, it may be reliable for other things, but it does not give good advice on the most important things. This must come from somewhere else, we must find a good source, we must search for wisdom.

How do we know when we are in touch with wisdom and not our mind? When the mind gives the answer to a question it

---

1. *Lā ilāhā illahāhu:* Breathe out *Lā ilāhā* through the left nostril, there is nothing other than You, O God, breathe in *illallāhu* through the right nostril, only You exist.

The recitation or remembrance of God which cuts away the influence of the five elements (earth, fire, water, air and ether), washes away all the karma that has accumulated from the very beginning until now; dispels the darkness, beautifies the heart and causes it to resplend.

The Kalimah washes the body and the heart of man and makes them pure, makes his wisdom emerge and impels that wisdom to know the self and God.

From: *The Map of the Journey to God,* by M. R. Bawa Muhaiyaddeen takes the long route around, it goes in circles until it finally lands somewhere. Wisdom's answer is immediate, without commentary from the mind, without the interplay of every circumstance to be taken into consideration before a decision can be made. Wisdom comes in a flash we should hold onto, if we let go of it the mind returns with its multiple choices.

We each have a spigot which releases the pure rain to wash away so many dramas, dilemmas and problems. This spigot releasing the wisdom and purity to resolve our difficulties depends on knowing how to get out of the way, a process which entails deep faith, no doubt whatsoever, and the disappearance of selfhood. When that happens things are available which have never been available before. We must have the faith that our ability exists, that there is a Creator who is deeply in touch with us, guiding us, giving us what we need. We need to know this, we need to know what is available, an aspect of our creation. Unlike any other creation, we were created with God's light, we are connected to His reality where everything is available, nothing is hidden. If we want explanations we must go there, we cannot be here and there at the same time. We have to choose where we want to be, do we want to exist in the context of the world or do we want to step into reality?

To step into reality we have to let go, we have to learn how to step away from the world, step out of the world. This cannot be something we play with, it must be what we do. We have to give up expecting anything from the world, give up wanting anything from it, relying on it, we have to give up all our attachments to it. Everything which binds us to the world keeps us from reality, everything we consider important in the world keeps us from reality. We have to live in the world without being here, existing here without expecting anything from it. Understand that we have a true nature and a false nature.

Religion has given us a level of understanding, a first understanding which knows how to deal with the world without relying on the mind. Beyond that, a second level, we have an understanding which develops the intention behind actions at that first step or level. Then a higher, a third level explains where that intention comes from, explains the qualities making up the intention. Finally, a fourth level of understanding gives us a gateway to reality.[2] All this is going on at the same time, we can be in all these places at one time, and we have to be appropriate for each of them at the same time. The first level does not talk about love, but love is an obligation at the fourth level. If we are not in a state of love we cannot go through that gateway, even if we are kings at the first level, the door to the fourth will not open without love. Understand the transformation of each level or stage, understand how to be appropriate for every stage we are in, above and below. We also have to be appropriate for those who are around us, even though what is appropriate for us may not be what is appropriate for them. We cannot fail to respect the state of someone else.

The ability to act correctly, to be appropriate in all this is subtle. On the Sufi path we have determined to be subtle, to understand the paradox of having two, three or four different things going on simultaneously, things which appear to be at odds with each other yet are not. If we cannot handle these subtle interactions we cannot be on the path. The path of truth is narrow, but a hair can be a bridge for an ant. We must be ants, very small, humble, with no self-importance if we are to understand the subtlety. Once we do, we fall into the awe and majesty of our Creator. He beckons us towards Him. We pray that we are made suitable to His call.

---

2. *Shariʿat:* The realization of good and evil and conducting one's life according to the good.
   Tariqat: Unswerving and complete acceptance of the good and carrying out of every action accordingly.
   Haqīqat: The realization of Divinity and the beginning of communication with God.
   Ma'rifat: The state of merging with God.
   From: *Four Steps to Pure Iman,* by M. R. Bawa Muhaiyaddeen

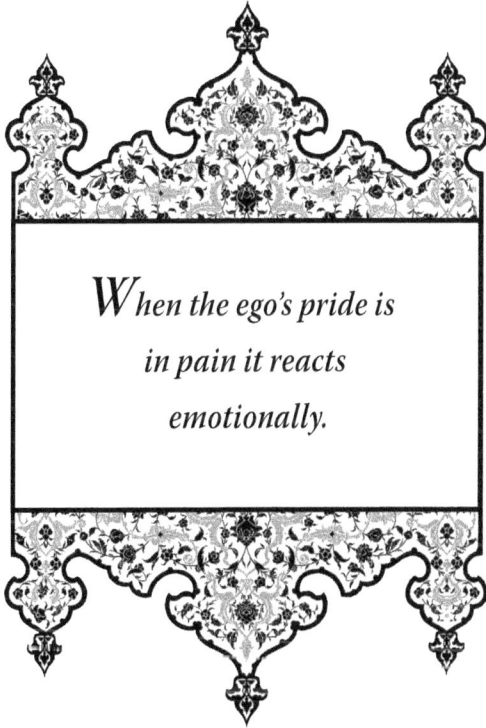

*When the ego's pride is
in pain it reacts
emotionally.*

Ego and Emotion

Some people call love an emotion, but if love is described as an emotion that makes it a lesser kind of love, a love which entails things that give us satisfaction. This kind of love, this kind of emotion is deeply attached to our ego, to our sense of selfhood which is so powerful within the ego with its built-in range of attitudes. The ego is proud of the self, protective of the self, and in its own way develops a sense of honor for the self. This does not mean that things developed by the ego have any ultimate reality, they merely exist within the self. When the ego's pride is in pain it reacts emotionally. Since the ego is tied to self-love, to love of the things it considers important for itself, if it sees its pride, its arrogance or importance attacked in any way, it reacts, it reacts in two ways.

First it feels pain, a pain similar to a knife wound. If our ego is sensitive, if we have not learned to withstand the pressure of daily existence, if we have had difficult experiences when we were younger, inadequate love and care, our ego might be starved for these lower emotions. An ego starved for these emotions can be a powerful agent searching for self-gratification, deeply in need of gratification. When these needs are unfulfilled in a basic way, it feels wounded, and when it is wounded it reacts like an animal. We should know this about ourselves, understand how and why we react when we feel someone has caused us pain, understand how

246	The Elixir of Truth: Journey on the Sufi Path

and why we react in response to someone we think has attacked us, on whatever level. We should also be aware of what we think of as an attack, aware of how sensitive we are, of what has made us so sensitive to a word, a look, or to someone else's lack of concern for us. Why are we offended, what do we take for offense, and when we are offended, what is our reaction?

The second way we react if we feel some sort of pain, is to develop a system to alleviate it, to bind the wound, stitch it up, stop the metaphorical bleeding, the infection. If we are ever going to make progress on this path we must specifically understand the qualities we use when our ego is hurt. Resentment might bind the wounds of that ego, that pain, and then if we lessen the importance of the person who hurt us, if we diminish him, we lessen our own pain because he was not significant enough, not worthy enough to cause us pain, and now we can begin to heal.

We do not heal by examining the pain, we heal by demoting the critic, by reducing the importance of the person who caused us pain. But as our resentment builds we are in pain more easily, our view of humanity shrinks, love for our friends and companions shrinks, our ability to interact with anyone else shrinks unless they overwhelm us with praise. This process can begin when we are young if we do not receive enough attention, if we do not have enough love, a process which builds through our life unless we catch it. We are negative in many situations to lessen the impact of what we expect, we anticipate pain and negate the experience before it occurs, we negate the people occasioning the experience before it occurs. By diminishing everyone around us and promoting ourselves, we create a reality where others have no emotional impact on us, they do not affect us, they are not worthy of affecting us, and we become cold, hard, like stone.

God sends people to this world who can bear the pain of the world, they bear it without complaint, without resentment, without a hateful reaction. These people are called saints, enlightened beings, friends of God. If we are in pain and fortunate enough to come before someone who takes on this pain, we can be relieved. We should know people who can bear the pain of the world, we should ourselves become someone who can bear this pain, have the ability to absorb it and deposit it in a place where it does not fester or put the world and its people in danger.

We should be able to understand the cause of this pain, understand how to defend ourselves from it, not react to it. It is easy enough to say detach yourself from the world, do not expect anything from the world, easy to say if you have no expectations you will not be disappointed. These are easy things to say, but we forget how tied we are to our ego, ignore that we have lost control of certain responses which can sneak up on us, catch us before we know it, and all our learned reactions are repeated as we feel cornered, waiting for attack.

We should know our own nature, study it carefully to see what we have learned to use as the remedy for pain. To be truly detached, to be free of this emotional self which is so overwrought and dramatic, so capable of overtaking us, we need the practice of prayer, the practice of negating the self on a regular basis. If we do not experience the negation of the self regularly, it is hard to avoid being overwhelmed by our emotional needs, our jealousy, our resentment, our self-glorification demanding all that.

Kings are no different from beggars in this way, everyone has that tendency. Those who have less of this are rare, those who have less of this can help us. We are not truly capable of giving until we overcome being negative and become positive instead. We must engage a genuine negation of the perceived self, a genuine negation of the egocentric self, of the base desires which function through that self. This can happen only by being aware of the self, by actively practicing its negation through different exercises of prayer.

The key to this understanding is that the I does not exist. If the I does not exist how can I hold all this garbage, if the I does not exist how can I be offended, if the I does not exist why do I need to protect myself, if the I does not exist why do I need to roar in defense of my inner being, if the I does not exist what is so important? The point is we have made that self, that ego, very large and we have to reduce it in size; this is what becoming small means. It means being able to disappear from everything reaching out for us. As we walk down the street and notice someone looking at us, we should not think it has relevance for us, we should not believe someone who cuts us off while we are driving is doing it deliberately, that anyone who honks his horn at us has some kind of relationship with us, they are people we have never met, never seen, yet we take their actions personally, seriously.

Our life is not personal in that way, it is not about ourselves and them, it is about God and ourselves. If we bring any other consideration into the equation we can end up with qualities which separate and destroy, we can end up in that egocentric situation which arises when we think we do not have the respect, love, admiration and homage our status deserves. This is difficult because we are not willing to think of ourselves as less than excellent, which is one aspect of our difficulty.

May God help us understand what resentment is, may He help us understand what jealousy is. To understand His qualities we need to understand our own qualities. May He keep us from being confused, may we see the hidden negative qualities within ourselves and tear them away. May He give us the strength to tear them away.

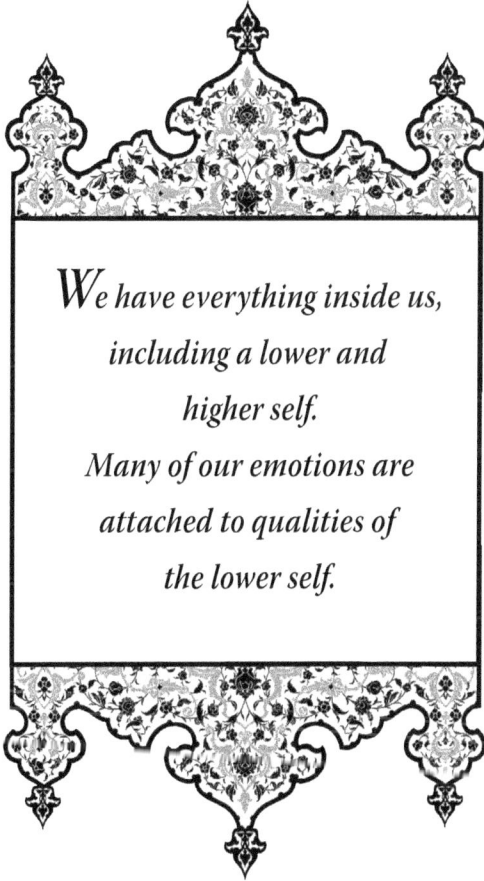

CHAPTER THIRTY-TWO

*We have everything inside us,
including a lower and
higher self.
Many of our emotions are
attached to qualities of
the lower self.*

Diseases of the Heart

Some people are good at receiving love but not very good at
returning it, giving it back. Why do people act the way they do,
what does it take to recognize how we behave? We seem to have only
a limited ability to recognize our own emotions, possibly because
emotions limit consciousness, they overwhelm consciousness in the
same way that alcohol and drugs do. Strong emotions overwhelm
our consciousness and keep us from thinking clearly, we react
through the emotion, the qualities this emotion brings with it.

We have everything inside us, including a lower and higher self.
Many of our emotions are attached to qualities of the lower self.
When these emotions take control of us the lower qualities are in
control, we learn to think this is who we are. Now we are confused,
we fail to see these qualities as a strange, invasive force making us
behave in unacceptable ways. We see these qualities as ourselves,
who we are, and this is just like consuming alcohol, it makes us
behave differently. There is nothing we can do about it until the
alcohol passes through us, until it no longer affects our capacity.

There are two considerations here, first, what these qualities
do to us, and second, what we can do to understand ourselves
better when these qualities rise up in us or in others. Many of the
difficulties have come because of what might be called diseases
of the heart, in other words a heart without purity, a failure of
purity which causes inappropriate actions. If we understood

appropriate actions completely we would recognize when we are being overwhelmed by something inappropriate; if we understood inappropriate actions completely and governed them, we would be able to stop them.

Let us think about this—psychology tells us to let our emotions out, to feel what we are feeling, express ourselves during the feeling. But if this is not really who we are, if it is merely a passing state, we can cause harm, especially if this is a thing of the moment, something which stays for an hour and leaves. Anyone who has ever had a fight with his wife and said things he regretted later understands what I mean, anyone who has ever had a fight with his child or a friend and said things he regretted later knows what I mean. We have all done that, said things we regret.

If we have control over our tongue and our words we know when we are overwhelmed, we know when it is time to take ourselves away from that situation, go to a private place, close the door until the emotion passes. It takes restraint and appropriate conduct, good qualities and respect for ourselves and others. When we practice that appropriate conduct with our language, our words, we bite our tongue before we speak. This means we stop ourselves from saying things we should not say, this is discipline, self-restraint, the ability to move away from a situation.

Why do we find ourselves in situations where we have to bite our tongue, why do we stumble into situations which make us angry with other people, what motivates this? There are so many reasons it is impossible to list them, we all have a different list, a different pattern most of which we acquire in childhood. There are so many examples. Think of someone with a cruel parent, so cruel that whenever the parent walks into the room the child is fearful, profoundly uncomfortable with a fear which becomes the ruling emotion of that life. As adults we might self-medicate with alcohol, but as children this is not possible. What can they do instead? They create another emotion to mask the unbearable fear, what alcohol does, something to deaden the emotion. But what emotion takes away fear? Anger, anger replaces fear of the parent, they are angry with the parent because it is easier to live with anger than with fear.

When we think about this, remembering a situation when we were fearful, we realize anger gives us more control than fear. Both are holes in the heart but they are different. As we are growing up whatever we do repeatedly becomes a pattern. Science recognizes that any action we repeat again and again creates a pathway in our brain stronger than pathways for things we have not repeated so often. Spaced repetition is a way to learn, the reason why multiplication tables are taught every day, again and again. By repeating something this way it becomes a pattern, we develop a pathway in the brain so that we do not have to think when someone says three times four, twelve jumps from our mouth, we do not have to work it out.

Thirty, forty or even fifty years later, if we have developed patterned responses to uncomfortable situations we go automatically to the most accessible groove in our brain when we are troubled. If anger is the most accessible pathway, when we are uncomfortable we become angry. What we learn as a child is written on stone, what we learn as an adult is like writing on water. Science talks about grooves in the brain, those grooves on stone are the same. Early childhood experience and the way we interact with our parents both have much to do with the way we grow up, with emotional responses when we are grown up.

Someone who has been loved as a child, with decent parents who have taken care of the child appropriately, is still not safe. There are the children on the street, situations outside the home we have to deal with. We have a variety of environments, those which are difficult can lead to the self-medicating responses of childhood. When we are adults we have similar things to deal with, still not easy if we do not know how to act. We have so many automatic responses to pain, to something we interpret as external attack, we believe pain gives us a license to react any way we want. We rationalize our action, that person caused me pain, we slap back automatically as if we were swatting a fly.

A sarcastic tongue can be automatic, emotional outrage can be automatic. How do we cure this in ourselves, how do we handle this and so many other responses from ourselves and others? There is a range of subtle things that might happen since anger is not the only response, it could be slander, it could be envy, resentment or scheming. Some people are obsessive about setting things right when they think they have been wronged. Any of this can occur if we look at situations inappropriately. Once we understand that people react because of their pain, once we understand that we react because of our pain, that these responses are merely to mask the pain, we know we have to find a remedy for all this pain.

What solves the problem, what corrects the inadequacy of the heart instead of masking it, making it worse? The answer is love, true love, real love. If we have been a stranger to love all our life we might be incapable of loving without the intervention of a loving being. One of the attractions of the truly great teachers is their extraordinary love; one of the attractions of a successful group is making us feel safe, allowing love to develop and grow.

Love does two things, it lets us understand the difficulties other people have, and it lets us understand what we encounter. Love teaches us to act in a way which is different from the responses of our usual pathways, our grooves. If a baby soils its diaper a rational adult who loves the child will simply clean it up, that is the end of it. Parents who scream at their children do not understand how to deal with them; when these children become adults they might not be able to handle anything without shouting.

The ability to absorb the pain which others direct at us is something we have to learn how to do. If we cannot absorb pain to a certain extent, always reacting as if it could be stopped by some external force, we are lost in our own emotional frailty. Pain does not come from the outside, although it can, I am not talking about the Cambodian holocaust or Rwanda, I am not talking about that, I mean the interactions in a theoretically peaceful society where we cause each other such pain. We need to learn how to associate with those who act inappropriately without letting their actions affect us.

There are different ways to do this. First is avoidance altogether, and severance of a relationship is sometimes the only cure. We need to be the doctor in such a situation. To reach the level where we can be the doctor in personal situations is difficult because we must first be our own doctor, heal ourselves. Once we are cured we can be the cure, we understand the pain and how to stop it.

How do we make love recognizable? In the civil rights movement Martin Luther King, Jr. did some amazing things within the movement itself, he made it nonviolent, pacifist. He did other things too. Look at some of the film footage showing African-Americans wearing signs that said "I am also a man". He embarrassed people into understanding things without being aggressive. If there was any humanity in those who saw that, it moved them, and if it did not move them it moved other people with the power to write laws and make changes.

We have to reach the humanity within each being, something which does not happen overnight. We touch it by getting each person to understand we are not invulnerable either, we recognize there is a problem, we understand they have a pain we can help them with, and this is what we can do with love. At a bookstore in Toronto someone recently asked me how he could help his alcoholic friend who was not listening to the advice he gave. When people are in a state like alcoholism, in any state of masking pain like anger, resentment, jealousy, obsession, any difficult emotional state, they cannot hear what we say. They are so engaged by their own situation they refuse to believe anyone can possibly understand.

What can we do with people in that state? Either we make a commitment to them or we do not. For some we cannot because it would be self-destructive, for others we might be nothing other than an enabler, but we can love them in an unconditional way without accepting what they do. If they trust us, if they know the love is real, the love is truly caring, they might begin to listen, then we can get them additional help. These things are not cured in a day.

In the way that people are physically addicted to alcohol, they are physically addicted to their emotions. These things have been ground into our brain so deeply that we have to recondition ourselves. Transformation is the hardest thing, and this path is all about transformation. Most people do not want to change, they do not want to change because they perceive themselves incorrectly, they see nothing wrong. The person who lashes out at us for some perception of inappropriate behavior thinks of himself as a little baby protecting himself with anger, he thinks of himself as the kindest, most lovable creature without recognizing he is now a monster protecting the baby. He is not that baby any longer, he walks around as a monster. We run into monsters, different degrees of monster we need to handle, both the outer monsters and the inner monsters.

May God help us all with that understanding, that patience, that transforming love for ourselves and those around us.

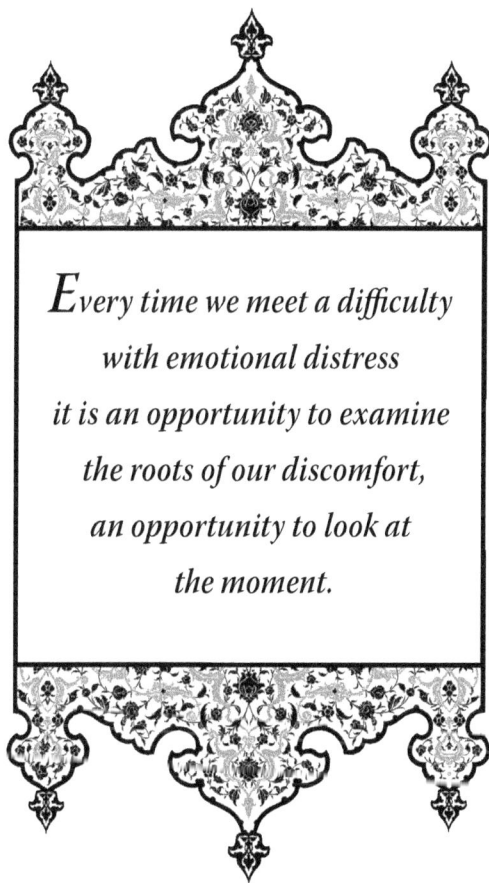

*Every time we meet a difficulty
with emotional distress
it is an opportunity to examine
the roots of our discomfort,
an opportunity to look at
the moment.*

Understanding the Spiritual Community

People in spiritual communities find it astonishing that they have to deal with the same problems in their community they have in the world, that people in their community have attitudes often found in the world, sometimes worse. Occasionally, the difficulties which come up in spiritual communities are more demanding than situations in the secular world.

When we look at the specifics of certain problems we often find the same script acted out in different circumstances. The facts do not usually determine what is going on, what is going on frequently has more to do with the emotional needs of those playing out their scenario. The facts might be a little different in each case, but reactions and interactions are often the same. There are two kinds of problems people have with each other, too much attention to the lives of other people and too little to their own. The spiritual path is one of self-discovery, the ability to know who we are, not to know who our neighbor is, what he is doing, how he is getting along. If our focus shifts from self-examination to what is going on with others, we have shifted from the spiritual path to something else, a path which is worldly, a path connected to motive, to power, the need to compare ourselves with others in order to feel that we stand up well in the comparison.

Comparisons we make between ourselves and others in the world are not the same as comparisons with reality. If we have no concept of reality, if all we know is the world, the only thing we can compare ourselves with is the world. Then when things in the world seem to be too different from ourselves we are frightened, unable to deal with the situation. We think we have to correct others, put others in their place, we have to reprimand, speak against, gossip or backbite to protect our integrity. But this integrity is not rooted in reality; the only way to protect this kind of integrity is with other things which are not rooted in reality, things which are lies, things without truth.

People on the spiritual path have to be aware of this. There are two things to think about here: first, we have to be aware of our own reactions to people who are different from us, and second, we have to be aware of the way we react to those who react against us because they fear our difference. Do we use the same tactics against them they use against us, or are we capable of behaving differently, sustaining ourselves in truth, in reality, in God's qualities?

When people say God resolves everything, this is open to some misinterpretation. When they say this they might mean He resolves everything as they want things to be resolved, yet what it actually means is that God resolves everything as He determines things should be resolved. There is a lesson here, when things are resolved as God wants them resolved and they do not meet our expectations, how do we deal with the problem? This is not God's problem, it is our problem, and the lesson is how do we handle God's resolution when it does not suit our requirements? How flexible are we in accepting the reality of the situation we find ourselves in, so different from our expectations, so different from the results we supposed?

Spiritual growth can take place here, growth which has to do with attitude, understanding our place in existence, our place in reality. If we misunderstand this point we will never correct our understanding, we will never engage the actual flow of things because we are swimming upstream, we keep struggling against what is going on, we have our own notion of the way things are supposed to be.

We are human, we have faults, we cannot help having expectations, but how do we respond when our expectations are not fulfilled? What happens when the road is rocky, what happens to our stability, to the ability to cope with things, does it fall apart? Do we become angry, resentful, jealous, do we have self-pity when things do not go the way we expect, or do we keep our faith when adversity comes?

This is what growth is about, what understanding ourselves is about. Every time we meet a difficulty with emotional distress it is an opportunity to examine the roots of our discomfort, an opportunity to look at the moment. Some say God gives difficulties to those He loves to bring them closer, bring them closer through adversity. One of satan's great tools is to make us feel comfortable, make us feel we have done what we need to do, make us feel we are exemplary. In that situation he has trapped us, we are stationary, no longer moving, no longer trying to make progress. This is a moment when God can shock us from that immobility, that place where we have stopped and come to rest.

We have to develop the right attitude about our life, understanding as we move along in any situation, including spiritual situations, that those who are not moving the same way at the same time cannot accept us. If some advance and others do not, those who do not often fail to understand why, then many worldly things come into play, resentment, jealousy and anger cause suffering. On the spiritual path, if we are more withdrawn from the world, if we pray more, do things others are not doing, they will have something to say. "Why do you need to do that, what's your problem, what's wrong with the way we have always done things?" "Why are you going through this? There's no need for it." "Isn't what we do good enough for you?"

For those who do not exist in reality, everything comes back to a concern for the self—they want everyone to focus on them, making their situation our situation. If we lose our focus we are just like them, just like those who point their finger, who gossip, who cannot understand that people who do different things are still perfectly acceptable.

As individuals we need to understand people can be different and acceptable, understand that our paths are not identical, the means of growth are not identical, people take a different length of time. The growth of an oak tree is not the same as the growth of a dogwood. Although both come from a seed and both reach maturity, their maturity is different, appropriate for each but different. We should be thinking about our own maturity, our own appropriate growth, not someone else's.

Religions are rife with schisms. When the prophets came people formed a community around them, practices began, then later arguments began, arguments about the word that came from God, each group insistent on its own interpretation, insisting that everyone follow them. Eventually, each group formed a church of its own or temple of its own as the original community split apart, each group claiming to be the only true way. This is history, claiming our way is the only true way, and it is still a problem right now, our way is the only right way, we will enforce it. The religions have this, our way is the only way, everyone has to do what we do or else we have to force it on them for their own good.

This means whatever is good for us must also be good for you, whatever you do that does not agree with us causes such disagreement and pain we have to impose our will. Not only does it cause us pain, but it also is also morally wrong; it is totally unacceptable and inappropriate behavior. Individual intolerance spreads to the community, to society, the religion and the whole country, but it starts individually. If people were tolerant individually the community would be tolerant, our community reflects the individual. A few individuals can change the community if they are sincere in truth, grounded in reality, God can manifest through them to influence a whole society. Such people have come at different times.

Each of us can be one of them, it is incumbent on us to be one of them. This is the work we have been given, to be exemplars of truth. Even if we sit in a corner without talking to anyone, just existing as truth in that corner, that vibration passing through us spreads to our surroundings and changes things. The world exists because of those who are the truth, when they no longer exist the world will no longer exist.

God created us and He created this world, He created the world so that He could experience Himself. God can experience Himself through human beings who exist with His qualities. This is the reason why creation exists, this is the responsibility we have in relation to creation. We each have a responsibility for what goes on around us, remembering that all those in the past who lived with His qualities encountered adversity. When we choose truth we should not expect to find everything peaceful merely because we are truthful.

Look at the lives of the prophets and their difficulties, look at the lives of the saints and their difficulties, were they deterred? If we are to reach that level, can we be deterred? Read Job, think about what he went through. Look at the life of Jesus, what he went through. Consider the life of Moses, the difficulties he had, the people he had to manage as he crossed the Sinai. Look at the life of Muhammad and the quarrels around him. Think about the lives of the prophets, the holy ones sent by God. They were neither spared offense nor deterred.

If we are so subject to the world that we need its respect, we cannot go on this path; if we free ourselves of the need for that respect, free ourselves of all the needs for those worldly requirements we have accumulated over the years, we can find our way on this path. Then we will understand the treasure, the true way, what really is available. If we have traded our inheritance for a few glittering things, for things we can feel and touch and see, we have lost our inheritance. We are not what we appear to be, we are not what we see with our eyes, smell with our nose, hear with our ears, we are other than that. Understand what that is, concentrate on that because to see with our inner eye takes great concentration, great focus. This is not a small thing, it is the most important thing in our life. May we each have strength for that focus, look at reality and see His splendor.

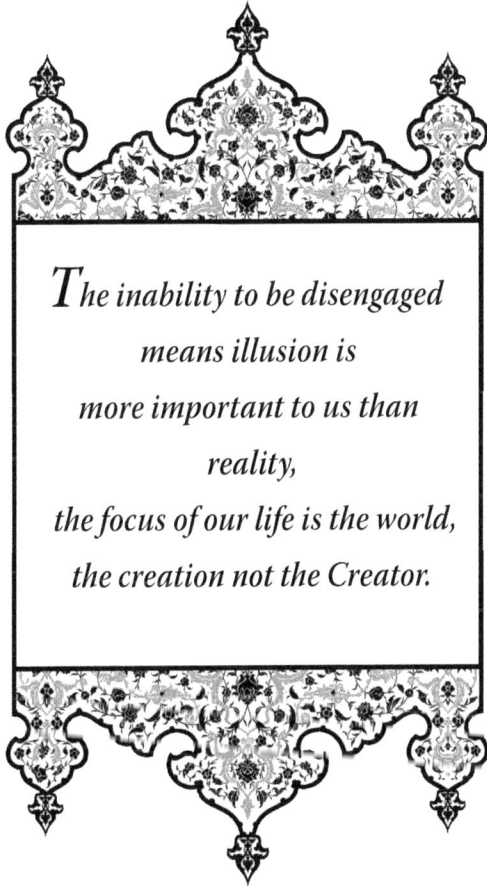

The inability to be disengaged
means illusion is
more important to us than
reality,
the focus of our life is the world,
the creation not the Creator.

Observing Ourselves

We have many different centers inside us, each of them exerting a specific effect at a given moment. These centers act in a way which resembles the elements, one emotional center is like fire, violent, consuming and caustic, another is like water, either soothing and cooling or overwhelming in its ferocity, like tempests of lust. All these things affect us differently, and if we do not have significant awareness of ourselves we can be taken for a ride on a roller coaster without control. Now a roller coaster does not have individual controls, it rides along on its tracks and we go with it. How do we get off a roller coaster once it is in motion? It is difficult, it could kill us—imagine jumping off, not a pleasant situation.

We should learn how to recognize the state we are in, improve it, make it the best we can, then find the right moment to change. We handle a situation within the parameters which present themselves, understanding we can only act within those parameters. We are not required to do the impossible, only the possible. If we interact with others and we are in a violent state, there is a good possibility violence will erupt. The best thing we can to do is to remove ourselves, go to a place where that mood will not affect others. Go to another room and close the door, know when we are capable of interaction and when we are not. We also need to learn what causes these explosive conditions so that we will not be subject to them, so that we can center ourselves in a peaceful way.

We should recognize that to make spiritual progress we have to be centered. This means not having a ready package of predispositions or attitudes which must prevail, not having rigid assumptions determining the way things must be. Being centered means being free within the flow of what presents itself, taking what is given as it comes, handling it, going along with a situation. Overreaction is one of the enemies we face, learning to treat each situation with an appropriate response is an acquired technique. Here is a version of Adam and Eve's story which makes a strong point about overreaction. God informs Adam he should tell Eve not to eat the fruit of a certain tree. Adam, to make sure she does not go near it tells her, "God said you should not eat anything from that tree, in fact, you should not even touch it." Satan approaches Eve when she is somewhere near the tree, walks towards it talking to her and makes her trip. She falls touching the tree.

The next day satan comes back suggesting she eat the apple. She says, "But Adam told me I cannot eat the fruit of that tree."

Satan replies, "Didn't Adam also tell you not to touch the tree?"

"Yes."

"Well you touched it, didn't you?"

"Yes."

"Nothing happened, did it?" And she eats the apple.

We can set people up for the possibility of failure if we exaggerate, we can set people up for inappropriate consequences if we do not treat them appropriately, if we believe we need to exaggerate to protect them. This happens when parents overprotect their children instead of being straightforward with them. They need to be told the truth about what is dangerous and what is not, without exaggeration.

We have to talk to each other without exaggeration, without blowing a situation out of proportion. If we tend to exaggerate we make things worse than they are, we make them more frightening because we have lost perspective. What we do outwardly we do inwardly too. If someone screams on the outside, inside that person's head someone is screaming in there too. If someone is outwardly paranoid, that person is in constant inner fear. We need to observe our own actions, watch what we do and how we react externally, this is a key to solving our inner problems.

Doubt is a problem that causes so much turmoil. Doubt comes in different forms and varieties. It might surface through the fear aroused by our expectations, when we have a list of expectations along with the accompanying fear that things will not turn out as we want them to, doubt creeps in. Doubt leads to misgivings, how can we change this, how can we make things work out the right way? This confused anxiety can lead to exaggerated actions, even chaos as we attempt to reconcile things.

There are stories we have heard to illustrate this, stories about being arrested, being caught, about individuals who get into much more trouble once they are caught. Suppose a boy steals a bicycle, a policeman comes to arrest him, he shoots the policeman. What causes this reaction? The boy stole a bicycle for which the punishment, the appropriate response is limited, but the response for killing someone is quite different. The boy's fear leads to confusion and chaos, loss of control, loss of appropriate behavior. We should know the same kind of thing can happen to us inwardly.

We need to be balanced to assess the relative importance of events, to know we cannot live with too many expectations or we will be disappointed. If we have an overload of expectations we are back on the roller coaster, a ride on the rails which are fixed, they are set in place. Once we are on we cannot get off. Function in situations which allow us to be disengaged, know how to disengage. Sooner or later everyone is disengaged from life, and when that happens everything in this life is over, but we may not be ready for this final disengagement. At least we should be ready for all the little disengagements which come along the way. If we are not, it means something in our life is inappropriate, we are clinging to things we should let go of, we are giving more importance to them than to reality.

The inability to be disengaged means illusion is more important to us than reality, the focus of our life is the world, the creation not the Creator. This is our state, our existence, everything is either masked or misconstrued, we do not see things as they are but as we imagine them to be. After all, we think we are looking after our duties, taking care of responsibilities, doing what we are meant to do, fulfilling our purpose, the reason we are here. This kind of thinking blinds us, we rationalize attachment, we rationalize our engagement with the things we take to be more important than our soul.

Religions function this way, religion makes itself more important than the relationship between man and God, religion becomes more important than the relationship between God and His people, the very thing the prophets of each religion came to establish. If this is happening in the religions with the consent of those who are learned in religion, think about our own life which is a religion too, our own life which is the story of the whole world. Our life is an example of everything going on, and everything going on is an example for us, the world is our translator of reality. We are meant to understand reality through our own experience, through what we see in life, we are meant to undertake an active, correct study of who we are within this span of our existence. If we keep dealing with what we think is arranged for us, we are locked in a groove, traveling on rails we cannot get off of. We are heading for the destinations these situations take us to, failing to realize we picked the route ourselves.

To go to that open space where nothing is predetermined, where reality exists, this is difficult. We have specific criteria identifying reality for ourselves, yet we must go beyond them, walk that tightrope to the edge of what we know. This is the straight, true path which is said to resemble the edge of a sword; we have to take ourselves beyond what we understand, beyond what we know. If we stay where we are comfortable, persisting in the place where we were raised, we repeat the same situations endlessly, not allowing any experience taking us beyond where we are.

The opportunity to learn, to have new experiences means we are sometimes put into situations which require the very thing we are trying to learn, qualities like patience, compassion or mercy. This is what happens in the world, those who favor God are favored by Him, those who are favored by Him have the opportunity to understand His qualities. If we want to learn mercy we will find ourselves in a situation where mercy is required, if we want to learn patience we will be given experiences that require patience. These are tests for us, can we actually be patient instead of just talking about it? Should we have discussions about patience and mercy or should we have these qualities? Some spend their life talking about it in study groups, meetings or forums where everyone is invited to think about such things.

We need to understand the difference between discussion and reality, then choose. Here is our choice, do we live with God recognizing His supremacy, or do we live trying to push the world in our direction? This is the choice we have to make, the choice we are given every day, every hour, even every minute and second. We are given this choice, do we walk the edge or do we run back to the world? We have to decide, can we be honest with ourselves, honest with everyone, or do we head for the security and comfort we are used to? Our comfort can be resentment, jealousy, feeling sorry for ourselves, feeling better than others, feeling a sense of differences among us, these are the places where the world is comfortable. We know that false comforts are not good for us. May God help us understand.

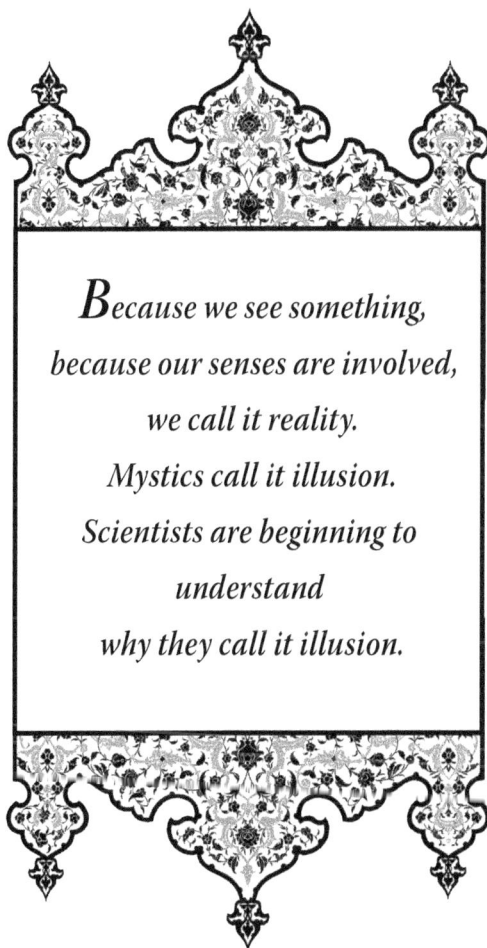

*Because we see something,
because our senses are involved,
we call it reality.
Mystics call it illusion.
Scientists are beginning to
understand
why they call it illusion.*

Quantum Physics and Free Will

The laws of Newtonian physics do not work when applied to subatomic particles. When we have an object we can see with our eyes and we throw it, we can establish where it was, when it reached its destination and how fast it was going. In the world of subatomic particles, if we know where they are we cannot say how fast they are going, if we know how fast they are going we cannot say where they are. This is Heisenberg's uncertainty principle which clarifies that we do not understand things in the same way in the subatomic world as we do in the atomic world.

There is more, subatomic particles do not react in the same way as atomic particles do in the world, things do not happen in the same predictable way. If we use Newtonian physics for subatomic particles we do not get the results we think we will. Spirituality is something like this, understanding reality is something like this. Once we understand that within what we see there are layers of things going on which we do not see, and when we realize these layers are the building blocks of what we do see, we can understand that what we are looking at is not really what we see, that there is so much more going on than what we see, that there is so much more to explain than what we see. What we see is shorthand for an inability to contemplate reality, a computed illusion we can engage.

Because we see something, because our senses are involved,

we call it reality. Mystics call it illusion. Scientists are beginning to understand why they call it illusion. We have different kinds of scientists, some who are engineers apply theoretical physics and chemistry to the gross world of the things we see with predictable results. Because their results are predictable they believe the theories are valid, and when they talk about theoretical physics they talk as if it had foundations we can grasp, but a theoretical physicist will not say that. They tell us we will not understand what they are talking about, no scientific lecture can convey what they are talking about, no advanced graduate student can understand what they are talking about because they do not themselves understand what they are talking about.

Those who are on the edge know that they do not know. As we get further in from the edge where the chasm beyond the edge is not visible, we think we are on solid ground. Most of those in the world walk around in illusion, believing they are on solid ground. Religion makes rules to have us believe we are on solid ground, religion says we have found the way, we know the answers, this is what it is. Follow our game plan, do not ask questions, do what you are told and we guarantee a place in heaven. Those who say this are the field workers, far from the edge.

In Newton's calculations the pull of gravity was considered to be an instantaneous response, something no one questioned until Einstein said nothing can travel faster than the speed of light, there cannot be instantaneous responses, there can be no response faster than the speed of light. Einstein concluded that gravity travels at the speed of light, but there is a time lapse, there is no instantaneous result. He questioned. Those of us who have looked deeply into our own existence have undertaken this questioning, not of the physics connected to the things moving around us, but of the physics connected to our very existence, the essence of our existence. Who are we, what are we, what are the laws governing us, how can we be in touch with who we are?

There are laws in this creation set by God, there are masters of the way who are certain of these laws, who tell us we have free will. What is this free will, the freedom to pick up a spoon and put it in a cup, does that signify free will? It must be deeper, is it the freedom to vote in a democracy? Are these things free will or are they just the random movements of a bag of protons, or as Rūmī would say, a bag of bones just floating through things and bouncing around. These are the things we touch, these are the things we do not touch, these are the things we decide. Is that free will or do we determine where we bounce?

Free will comes down to a simple choice we make, do we believe there is a supreme power governing all that exists or do we deny this? If we believe in a supreme power governing everything, do we attempt to align ourselves with the will of that supreme power, the way of that supreme power, or not? This is the extent and range of our free will. What are the consequences for us? Everything flows, and we decide whether we are going to move with the flow or fight against it. That is as far as we can go, it is a major step towards aligning ourselves with the Supreme Power, quite an adventure. Understand its magnitude, understand that the reward of going along with this flow is understanding it, becoming part of it. The penalty for not choosing to be in the flow is not knowing, not being part of it, excluded from the grace of reality. This is the choice we have been given, this is our free will.

That supreme eternal power has sent us instructions, how to be involved in this flow, instructions which come from divine texts, from those sanctified beings put in our midst who are clear and pure enough so that the will of everything which exists, the will of eternity, the will of that one power driving everything actually flows through them. They let us witness this and mimic what they do so that we can also be clear, purified, brought to that space where we are with the flow of things.

The laws governing societies, governing the world, even portions of the religions, are not necessarily laws given to us by the Eternal One. His laws are the nature of things, what reality is, the reality we must bring our own self to. But it is difficult for many reasons, we have established within ourselves what we consider common sense, what we like and what we do not like, the way we see things, the way we think things ought to be. We come to the table conditioned to expect things a certain way. As long as we hold onto these expectations they become veils blocking our ability to see the truth. Unless we can submerge everything we have imagined, take it all back to zero and come without expectations, shake ourselves free of the preconditioning, remove everything we hold sacred which is not truly sacred, when we stand before the truth, we will not recognize it.

There is a story about Khidr Nabī, the eternal prophet who walks the earth. Once there was a man who had a firm intention to find Khidr Nabī. He sat in meditation for days, weeks, months and years, until finally he had a vision of him which he sketched for himself on a piece of paper, folded it up and put it in his pocket. He said, "Now I am ready to find him."

Some years later someone approached saying, "I am Khidr Nabī, your intention has born fruit."

The man took the piece of paper from his pocket, looked at his picture which did not match what he was looking and said, "No, you are not." He turned and walked away.

This is the story of many people who are unwilling to give up images they believe to be sacred, unwilling to empty themselves when they go in search of truth. They want the truth to fit their own definition, and if it does not they deny it. The hardest part of this journey is coming to the realization that we know nothing, that when something of value is brought to us, we will not be able to recognize it from anything we have learned in the past, unless of course, we were raised by enlightened beings.

The rules or laws which work in spirituality, in the world of reality, are different from the rules which work in the world. In this world we need to do basic things, provide for ourselves, our families, have a job, be able to work, acquire things to provide for the physical body. These are essential, if we do not take care of them our body will wither and fade, but in the world of spirituality it is the opposite. On the path to reality we have to learn how to give up the things we accumulated in the world, give up our attachment to them, making sure we do not pick up things as we go along, things which keep us from moving forward. The things we pick up, the things which keep us from going forward are sometimes called karma. We need to be careful not to pick up karma as we walk this path, carefully removing the karma we have already acquired.

What is karma, how does it work? There is a story about a great, holy being in the north of Sri Lanka which tells us something. It seems there was a man who went around town slandering the wise man, saying vile things about him. One day the saintly man met the slandering man in the street, stopped and gave him fifty rupees, a lot of money at the time. This shocked the man, he knew what he had been doing, "Why are you giving me this money?" he asked.

The wise man answered, "I know what you have been doing, I wanted to thank you for it."

"Why?" asked the other man.

"By slandering me you have taken karma from me which has been added to yours. Karma has been taken from my balance and added onto yours. I thought I should reimburse you for this great service."

This was the explanation of the great being, teaching us how we pick up karma, how subtle it can be. If a word comes from our mouth which is inappropriate to the flow of things we pick up karma, if we do things which harm the flow we pick up karma. Everyone we see before us is in the flow—if we do something to make their path more difficult we are interfering with the flow, we pick up karma. Every bit of karma we pick up we have to get rid of later. This is one of the hardest parts of the path because we have all accumulated karma. Since we were babies we have been deceived, we have been lied to, we have been told things which are untrue. We trusted what we were told and passed it on to others. We were not only deceived, but we were also the deceivers, accumulating karma even in our innocence.

What happens to most people when they understand their karma, when they hit this wall of realization, they feel pain and regret. Now several things can happen, one is they get overwhelmed by the pain and regret, run away altogether, going another way, dropping their search, or they have the courage to go through the valley of pain and tears. It takes courage to face the demons they have accumulated and dispensed, courage to face the things they have done, to continue knowing what they have done.

Everyone hits this wall, the place where we have to make a decision, carry on, break through, or accept mind and imagination as more important than reality, keep doing what we have always done. There are many reasons connected to our egocentric sense of self, why we choose to keep doing what we have always done. Instead of trying to find God we make ourselves god, we equate our own will with reality, a phase of being blocked by preconceptions which can happen at any level.

When we are afraid to go forward or too frightened to move away, when we see that chasm we walk along and do not know if there will be something there to hold us up for the next step, when we get to that point, this is the place where life changes, where we change. This does not happen only once, it happens every day, again and again, it never stops. There is a story about a great saint who was asleep and he was on his way to the heavens. As he was about to reach the finality of things his wife ran into the room and began to shake him, screaming his name. He heard his name and turned back to look, he was drawn back.

There are so many challenges, so many of them feel appropriate, feel like things we should do, but in the end nothing exists but God, everything else is illusion. Until we truly believe that point, until we are free of attachment, we face that chasm every day. May we face it with courage, may we face it with appropriate actions.

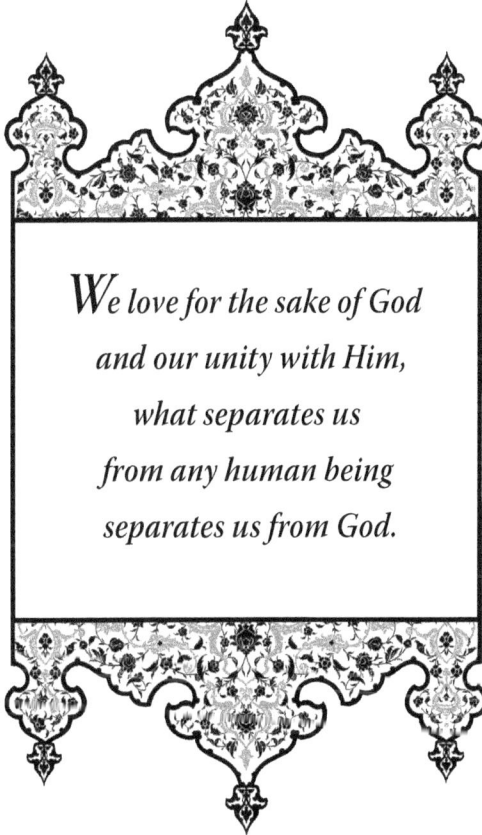

*We love for the sake of God
and our unity with Him,
what separates us
from any human being
separates us from God.*

A Code of Conduct

Chivalry was a traditional code of conduct shared by the east and the west, a core of understanding in allegiance between knights and kings, a code of conduct similar to the Sufi code in some ways. This includes the understanding that we bring into action the things we talk about, the things we believe in. The world talks about love, yet no one is actually loving, and we are supposed to put our beliefs into action. Since the practice is so rare, those who want to engage in specific codes of conduct sometimes form small groups, like King Arthur with a round table and his knights, or like Sufis who meet with allegiance to certain teachers or sheikhs.

There is a core of allegiance to each other among the members of such a group, a declaration of love and attempts to bring that love into action. Marriage is a version of this, the smallest group pledging love and allegiance which tries to bring this into action, a simple institution with that simple understanding. It has been said that marriage is half our religion. There are many ways to understand this, but we can take it as a subtle understanding that only God exists. If God alone exists anything we think of as separate takes us away from knowing we are part of everything. As a part of everything we are part of that all which is One; when we separate ourselves from anything we lose our connection to this One. If we learn how to be one with a spouse we are on that path, the path of learning to be one with those we encounter, one, not separate.

The knights of old were ready to give their lives for each other, just as the ancient dervishes were committed to each other and to their sheikh. Commitment to a small group is important, but a problem can arise when the group separates itself. They might come together with wonderful ideals until they are institutionalized, then to protect the institution ideals fade as they come into conflict with other groups. They adopt a sense of exclusivity, their religion, their path has exclusive access to truth, their way alone leads to reality, to a relationship with God.

First we need to practice love, understand it, understand what happens when there is real joy among people. All the religions talk about deep love among disciples, among apostles, dervishes, knights, Chassidim, whomever. There are examples in every faith of what happens with the expression and practice of love, stories about people who cross over the bridge of that exclusivity. Saint Francis of Assisi, we are told, walked a great distance to meet Salāhuddīn for a loving exchange with him. Today there is a movement among religions to cross the bridge and recognize the legitimacy of personal faith in different forms. The refusal of many to grant legitimacy to different faiths causes so many problems, especially when it ends in the degradation of others as inferior, as less than human, giving themselves permission to take whatever action they choose.

When we establish conditions which encourage conflict, when we cannot love, we damage our capacity for reality, we damage our ability to make progress on the path towards God. Once we create situations in which we are inclined to be hateful we create a place within ourselves for this attitude, for this emotion to exist. If we think a hateful or contemptuous reaction is appropriate in certain circumstances, understand that who we are, that what we are is what we carry around with us. No matter where our anger is directed, no matter how righteous or appropriate we think that anger is, it is still anger, we have become vessels transporting anger not love.

'Alī, the son-in-law of the prophet Muhammad, was once in battle and about to kill an enemy when that enemy spat on him.

Immediately 'Alī dropped his sword. Amazed by this, the man he was about to kill asked him why he had stopped. 'Alī answered, "When you spat at me I became angry—I came here to defend our city when it was attacked, a just and appropriate cause, but now I was ready to kill because I was angry, that was inappropriate." According to the story, the enemy was converted by 'Alī's explanation. What we need to understand is the nature of anger, why we hold onto it, what it does for our ego, our intentions, how it makes us feel, why it makes us feel that way.

We will probably all encounter difficult people we should not interact with. It is better to end the interaction than to become angry, conclude a situation which cannot be handled and let it go, understand the state of love, understand why we love. We love for the sake of God and our unity with Him, what separates us from any human being separates us from God. We should unlearn separation, learn how to be inclusive. We have an undifferentiated soul that comes from God, we are all created this way. How can we see the sameness within us, how do we learn to care for each other as we care for ourselves? We can do this by recognizing the sameness, if we do not see the oneness we cannot understand, if we cannot see others as ourselves we cannot treat them as ourselves. We can do this by realizing there are no differences although the world keeps creating them, differences of race, language, religion, wealth, status, education, power, differences created by what we have or do not have.

For our own safety we should learn to avoid certain situations, understand that just as some have a broken arm or leg, others have diseases of the heart which need to be fixed, diseases which are not normal. When we see it this way, when we recognize the sameness in each other, begin to have different relationships with people something extraordinary can happen. When we discover unity a certain glory occurs which we are allowed to participate in, there is a grace which sets the limited self aside and places us deeply in the undifferentiated self existing within us all.

This expansive process usually starts with those who are in our lives. It is not an accident that we have some contact with them, we should not treat it as such. Those we meet are the people we can help, we can interact with and love, we all have this grace. We are to deal with who and what we are, love what we have been given, love what is put before us. We should not look at the plate of the person beside us, we should eat the food on our own plate, take the serving which is our own.

Once we look at someone else's share we lose the focus on love, we engage qualities making it difficult for love to exist. When we wonder why someone else has something we do not, doubt creeps in, when we ask why, we doubt the perfection of God's plan for us, we lose our connection to Him, our love for Him, our gratitude to Him, we lose our path to Him because doubt and the way do not coexist. They exclude each other, doubt takes us away from God just as it takes us away from each other. We need to be loving, we need to be in love, find ways to be in love, situations of love, things which offer love. We need to care for others and forget about ourselves, as we forget about ourselves our attention can be focused somewhere else, some place where the opportunity to love exists.

There is a special kind of relationship in a special place, God's cornucopia where there is always more to give. God keeps giving, when we are part of the longing to give, when that is our intention He offers His abundance. We should go to this place where there is such joy it brings tears of gratitude, exultation, we are safe, protected, among people with whom we share the reality and unity of existence. This is a reason why people come together, a reason why people love. That pure love is the door opening a pathway to God, our supreme treasure who is available to us as we make ourselves available to Him. May our hearts open, may this love be the intention behind our actions in the world.

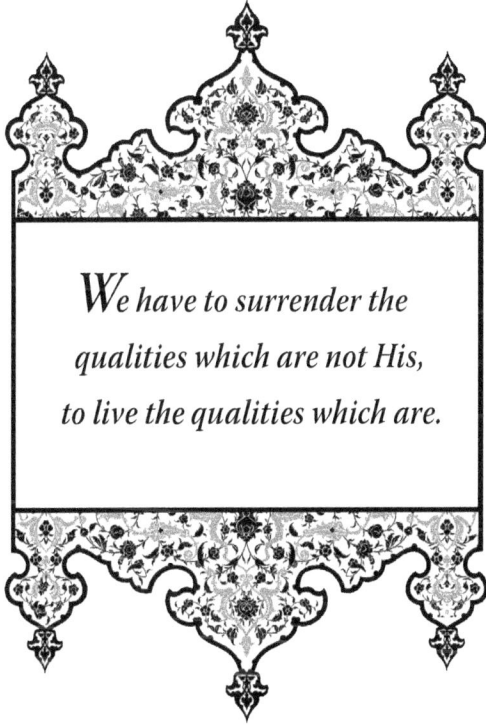

We have to surrender the qualities which are not His, to live the qualities which are.

Resonance and Light

Recently we met two people who were believers in God, believers who wanted to be with other people who are enthusiastic about their belief. Because we all shared this enthusiasm the experience was beautiful, rewarding, we shared common feelings, emotions and understanding. There was so much of this communal understanding it brought unity; when there is unity God joins us because He wants us to be one. If we do what He wills, His will is to be with us. Why do we have such meetings, why do we come together? We do this to understand how to align ourselves with His will, something which allows His qualities to come among us, to be with us so that we can engage His qualities shared with all creation.

Here is a Creator who is compassionate, here is a Creator who is merciful. What has He done for His creation? He has let us know compassion and mercy. In His mercy He has given us the ability to experience compassion, in His mercy He has given us the ability to experience mercy, and what happens when we taste this food of His, what happens when we accept these gifts? We come closer to Him, and by coming closer to Him a new field of vision opens for us, new ways to see are opened, the love which is our natural state begins to grow. Every time we meet we bring another log and add it to the fire, we make the fire burn higher, we make that thing which burns inside us, the love which grows inside us, we make it burn brighter as we come closer to Him. With the certitude that He is with us, that we are with Him, we are moved with the knowledge that our Father is with us, we are with Him, and then we are stronger, more steadfast in certitude.

When we sit together sharing space, sharing the air, focusing on the same point at the same time, when we talk we are not thinking, when we listen we are not thinking, we are sharing what is coming through, what is given. We have removed ourselves from involvement with anything but Him. He is providing this moment for us—the miracle of letting Him provide for us is being shared. When we think we can push and pull the world to make it do what we want we are deluded in thinking we can provide for ourselves. When we are stuck in that place which thinks we are the providers, we are the doers, we are the knowers, we cut ourselves off from Him.

We need to understand our state, understand simultaneously the difficulty and glory of it, we need to understand what He allows us to do and what He has kept for Himself, understand what is right and what is wrong, then choose the correct path. Those who have surrendered to a teacher, a sheikh, or a guru, need to understand what this word surrender means. Surrendering has strange implications for us in the west, but there is much more here than we think.

When a child is angry with its parent or a parent is angry with its child, what happens? A separation occurs along with the pain of separation, the hurt felt because of something that happened, something the child or the parent did. Now how is this hurt reconciled? It is reconciled when one of them surrenders to the other, when one of them forgives the other. Surrender permits forgiveness, surrender and forgiveness together permit unity. When a wife fights with her husband or when a husband fights with his wife, they need reconciliation to restore unity. How is this unity established? When their wills become aligned then unity is restored.

This is the way it is among human beings, among men and women, and it is also the way between man and God, between man and his teacher. We have been given the explanation that God's will is manifest through certain qualities. When we align ourselves with these qualities we engage Him, when we are not aligned with

His qualities we are separate from Him. We have to surrender the qualities which are not His, to live the qualities which are. When that happens we engage Him? He can show us what He is like, we have not stopped ourselves from uniting with Him. Real peace in this world comes only when that alignment occurs. There is a stillness in real peace, a quiet which lets us hear the resonance which is His.

Think of our bodies for a moment. We are made up of various elements, various things which combine to create us as functioning beings. We have been told by the prophets and friends of God that a particle of the eternal has been placed inside each of us, a tiny particle within our heart given to us by God, yet we are so overwhelmed by those elements we have lost the ability to comprehend that particle which is from God. Our work in this world is to focus on that bit of ourselves which is His, then we can emanate His resonance. Everything we see has a certain resonance. A scientist can explain the different vibratory nature of things. All creation has a specific vibratory nature; the Creator has a vibratory nature, a resonance. Are we interested in the resonance of creation or in the resonance of God?

We appear to have many choices in our daily life, many choices as we go through our existence, but choices are, in fact, quite limited. We can choose either the world and all that it implies, or we can choose God. Any choice we make associated with the world is not choosing God. Any time we choose God we forget the world. How do we choose God, how do we come to the point where making the choice for God is simple instead of a struggle? We need a certain attitude about our lives, an attitude which must be made easier. If we think life is a struggle, if we think life is difficult, if we think we have to use our effort merely to maintain our own existence, we do not have time to think about God. But if we go through our lives with ease, without difficulty, without being so focused on things which appear to be problems, it becomes easier to choose God.

How do we cultivate an attitude which makes this possible when there are countervailing forces that make us think another way? Our ego tells us we are great, we can accomplish things, we can take on great difficulties and overcome them, we can move things, we are capable of important decisions, overwhelming decisions. Either we move into an understanding of ourselves or we pull away from the state necessary for involvement with Him. Sometimes, we deliberately put ourselves into situations which are difficult, which we find complicated.

We need to move with ease through the world, we need to travel the path of least resistance. The world offers us many choices, and occasionally we decide we want things which do not come easily, which might not be meant for us. Take for example the mayor who wants to be governor, the governor who wants to be president, the president who wants to be emperor. The inability to be satisfied with our own position, the inability to be satisfied with the portion we are given is an obstacle on His path.

There is a story about a poor man who used to earn five rupees a day. At the end of each day he would spend the money on food and fruit which he shared with his friends, then go to sleep at night, wake up the next day, go to his job chopping wood, earn five more rupees and do the same thing again every day. There was a miser who lived up on a hill, a very rich man who could see how the poor man lived. He said, "I don't understand how this man can spend all the money he makes every day. I don't even give myself a rupee to buy fruit because it will decrease my wealth, the most important thing I have."

He went to a wise man, complaining about what he saw, and the wise man said, "Well, do what I tell you and see what happens. Put ninety-nine rupees in a bag, throw it into the poor man's hut, then go back up to your villa and watch."

The next morning the poor man woke, found the bag with the rupees inside. He began to count, "My God," he said, "You have been so generous to me, You have given me ninety-nine rupees, I'm a wealthy man. If only You had given me one more, I would have a hundred, I would really have some wealth in this world." After that, the man could no longer spend money on his friends, could no longer buy food to give away freely. He was too anxious, too worried about the little bag of money he kept trying to increase to a hundred rupees. When he had one hundred he wanted two hundred, when he had two hundred he wanted three hundred, a never-ending story.

When do we say enough? When do we offer our praise to God who has given us such an overwhelming portion we can only praise Him for His kindness, for His grace, when are we in a state of complete gratitude? We can only be in that state if we decide to be in that state, when we are no longer grasping for more, when we are satisfied. We need to understand this kind of satisfaction, we need to understand what His grace is, what He has to give. In a profound way we are all the same even though we do look a little different, we have been raised in a slightly different way, we have circumstances which are a little different. Each creation is a little different from every other, yet if we spend our time looking at the differences we will never understand His point. If we look at each other saying this one has that, that one has this but I do not, we enter the arena of comparisons. Once we begin comparing we are lost, there is no end to it, no end to wanting more than we have.

It is easy to accept praise. When we praise certain people we can get them to do anything we want, praise is their food. If we were to blame them as we praise them they might kill us. Praise and blame are perceived as happiness and sorrow. We should recognize a place where neither praise nor blame matters, where the only thing that matters is His love for us and our attempt to change our life.

Attitude comes mainly from being either positive or negative. We need to place ourselves in positive situations, we need to look at things and see what is positive about them. We should be for things not against things, we should move away from situations which makes us negative and move towards those which makes us positive. Isn't being with God a joy, isn't remembering the prophets a joy, isn't thinking about the masters of wisdom a joy?

The immensity and wonders of creation should give rise to great joy, yet for some reason we acquire difficulties which weigh us down. We must unburden ourselves, we have to give our burdens to someone. God will take them from us, He will gladly take what we do not want without asking anything in return.

We have been told about the importance of charity. This point needs to be understood as well as the point of our relationship with Him—His relationship with us is the same as our relationship with others. Since His relationship with us mirrors our relationship with others, if we expect certain things from Him we should look at ourselves to see who we are. We create our relationship with God through the relationships we create with each other. Understand that His judgment is different from the world which rewards those who have accumulated titles and wealth. God's judgment rewards those who have accumulated love.

Who are we? Are we more beautiful when we come into a situation or when we leave it? Do people applaud our entrance or our exit? Are people happy to see us or happy to see us go? What is the condition of our life, what is the relationship we have with each other? Remember that God has put Himself in each of us. We must not forget this means every time we interact with each other we are interacting with God.

Do unto others as you would have done unto you, that is a basic principle in all the religions. Who are you, who are the others, how do we need to act? First, how do we need to act with ourselves, do we have appropriate respect for that God inside ourselves? Where do we go, where do we stay, what sort of situations do we stay in, what sort of thoughts do we allow ourselves to think? Once we are appropriate with God in ourselves, can we accept God in other people, can we be their witness for what is inside them, can we look into their eyes as if we were looking into our own, can we see ourselves in others? Are we separated by our skins or are we integrated in the best way, could we live in each other's skins? When there is a moment we are so close we feel there is no separation, there is only one, He has joined the party. He has come among us because we are one with each other, completely together, not separate, and when we are not separate from each other, He is not separate from us.

We must not be separate from Him, we must not be separate from each other. When we come together in small groups, when there are only a few of us, we can look at each other, we can acquire the ability to be aware of each other. God is simultaneously intimate with each of us and with all of us. We need to remember He is no more intimate with me than He is with you, an intimacy shared in an absolute way, beyond imagination in its glory for you and for me.

If I think God is more intimate with me, is more glorious for me than for you, I have cut myself off from you and from Him, these are not the conditions He operates under. He operates the same way with all of us; when we are all one we are with Him. We have to understand this explanation, we have to pray to find Him in each other, find Him in the gifts we offer each other. The best gift we can offer each other is the gift of God who exists within us, who wants to come through us to each other, allowing us all to see the truth of ourselves in Him. The great mystery is the mystery of man and God, the truth which exists in each of us. We all walk around with that mystery, we are as important as anyone else. If we believe God separates us, what chance is there He will be among us?

Every religion, in its time, has moved towards and away from the understanding of oneness. When understanding becomes more institutionalized and restrictive it begins to separate people, yet there is a path of love which opens doorways beyond our comprehension. God is beyond comprehension, if we try to think about Him we limit Him, and we cannot place limits on Him. Stop thinking about Him, just let Him show Himself to us, let Him show the glory our eyes can see and our body can feel. This happens when we stop interfering, when we stop imagining, when we stop supposing and learn to walk His way, without expectations or conditions.

Expectations keep us from movement. If we want something, if we strive hard for it and do not receive it we are disappointed, a disappointment which ends in negative energy. If we have no expectations we cannot be disappointed. We need to learn how to have no expectations, how to do what we need to do, treating this place as a school, as a test for us, a test to learn how to know God, a test whose results are not in our hands but in His. He only has to say, "Be!" and it is, while we struggle and struggle to make something happen. We think we can force that thing into existence, then when it does not happen we are disappointed, when it does we are happy. It is not the outcome God tests us on, it is the way we go about our life.

They say it is not about whether we win or lose, it is about how we play the game. This is also one of God's rules, our life is not about what we accumulate, our life is not about the status we earn, not about the titles we receive, our life is about the way we live it. What are the things we do as we go through our existence, what is our relationship with other people like, how much love do we walk around with, how much love do we take from place to place?

This is the reason for the existence of the great teaching masters who came to teach us a state of being, they came to give us an example of someone who is not attached to coming and going, to the status and titles of this world. In their presence we feel a joy we cannot comprehend away from them, the awe that such teachers exist. Think about such awe, think about being so overwhelmed we drop all thought of everything going on in our life because the being in front of us is so amazing, so beyond comprehension it comes close to shutting our mind off altogether.

On the path to infinity we have an infinite number of thresholds to cross. Each one beckons us to call it home, yet if we decide to stay at any one of them we stop being a pilgrim and become a defender of thresholds. What does this mean? It means that every time we have reached a new plateau, every time we catch a glimpse of grace and say I've got it now, we have stopped. We need to have the steadfast humility which reminds us that the road is long, the journey continues, there is no time to stop, we must keep going.

The fire of love is an interesting fire. That fire does not burn our good qualities, it burns our desires which cannot survive this light of love. When we expose animals to fire they run, and the animals inside ourselves run away when the fire of love burns near them. They are ashamed, frightened of the things they have done, embarrassed when true love is there. They run, only the part of ourselves which tolerates light remains. Let us build a large fire of love, let us come close to the fire, then when we have the urge to run let us stand still. The animals inside will run away, but that part of us which is one with the light will stay. May we know that inner place which accepts the light of reality, which is one with that light. May this light illuminate our lives. May we have the courage to stay in that light.

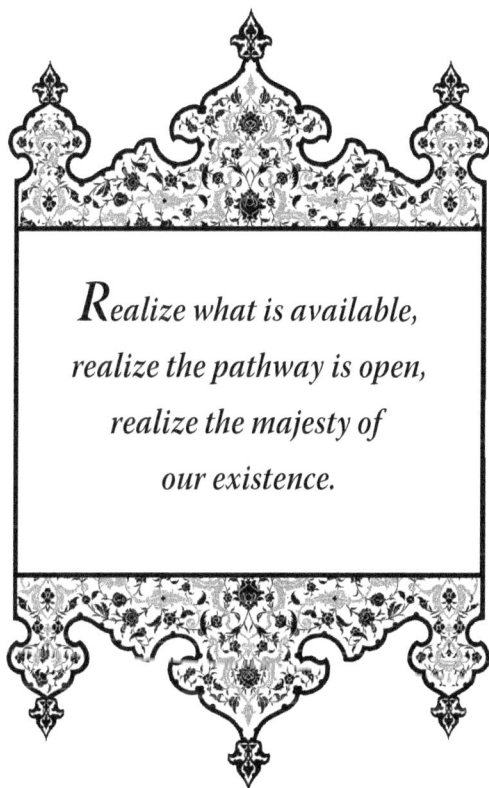

*Realize what is available,
realize the pathway is open,
realize the majesty of
our existence.*

Beyond Attachment

God is beyond estimate, beyond thought process, beyond our ability to comprehend, beyond anything we see or hear. God is greater than our imagination, wider than our vision, beyond any of our senses. He is beyond what we touch, feel, see, hear, smell, taste, God is none of that. But if we exist within such things we are separated from Him: we should ask God to separate us from all that separates us from Him, ask to be separated from our attachment to hearing, to sight, to our sense of smell and touch, to be separated from anything which separates us from Him. We should ask to be separated from the imagination which produces images that are not real, from any thought process which separates us from Him.

This prayer must be recited within our inner depths, it must be genuine, at the pure level called sincerity. It is difficult to reach the station of sincerity when we are attached to outer things. Attachment negates our sincerity, inserts a motive which separates us from the intention to be attached to God; understand the distinction. We need to find time each day to separate ourselves from this worldly existence, a separation deep enough to eliminate all the outer distractions at the surface.

When we look at an ocean we see constant movement, even turbulence. Everything passing over the ocean affects its surface, but below, very deep, there is a stillness, a quiet different from what happens at the surface. Most people in the world are surface dwellers, but our consciousness should function beneath the surface of illusion. We need to dive deep into a place where the attachments and separations of the world leave us. We have to find that space within us, accept that this space exists, at the same time understanding we also live in the world.

The dolphin living in the ocean must come to the surface to breathe, and yet it has to dive down to eat. To discover our own true sustenance we have to learn how to dive, how to escape the surface, to find that place not affected by what is no the surface. When we live at the surface every motive connected to selfhood tries to manipulate what happens, searching for gratification of animal instincts and the self.

There are things we need just to maintain existence, we need food and shelter, essentials to take care of. We have families and responsibilities which require effort at the surface. As we make these efforts we are subject to the fascinations, the pulls, the attachments and influences of all of the surface things. We need to be aware of this while remembering there is another place beyond the surface world, the world of sincerity, truth and reality. We have one foot in each world.

It is up to us to find the pathway to this other space, up to us to enter the open door. We should learn how to approach the door, realize it is open and follow the instructions given, learn how to enter the open door. Begin by asking sincerely that the pathway be open for us, by knowing the pathway is open. The great teachers all say stop knocking on open doors. Realize what is available, realize the pathway is open, realize the majesty of our existence. Get rid of the idea that we are less than majestic, unworthy, not His child, and understand the glory of a human being, the greatest of God's creations. As we contemplate the majesty of God's creation, recognize the majesty of its Creator, recognize we are dependent beings, dependent on Him, our Creator.

We live our life without apparent effort. He has given us the ability to intend movement and our hands move, He has given us the ability to open our eyes and we see, He has given us all that. God shows us what He can do when He wills a thing, but we lose sight of

His gifts. They seem so ordinary because everyone has them, they are available to all of us, as God Himself is. Without appreciating His availability to each of us, we will not understand.

To be in that station of sincerity we must have this understanding deep within ourselves, not only do we have to be separate from everything which separates us from God, we also have to be separate from everything which separates us from our fellow human beings. Once we have separated our sense of distinctiveness, that need to be different, we can move towards the next step, union at the level of sincerity, the level of love.

They say love comes first to us and then to God. There is a tradition which tells us that half our religion lies in our marriage. Understand what this means: marriage is a union between two people, a place to understand oneness, the avoidance of separation, it is a place for this understanding to grow. The understanding must also spread through the world, it must also be available in the world. We need to end resentment, end jealousy, we need to end paranoia and any sense of difference, these things must be eliminated as a reflection of surface attachments, things which affect us if we are not in the station of sincerity, if we are not in communion with reality. These emotions can only arise when we are separated from reality.

Part of us exists in reality and part of us does not. When we live at the surface, that part of us which does not belong to reality is dominant, but when we go deep within we end the separation, the truth of who we are becomes gradually known. As we glimpse more and more of the truth we are more comfortable, we begin to understand, melt into it, become one with it, then the duality of surface existence disappears as we disappear. This path can lead to a kind of craziness or it can lead to truth, depending on how we handle it, depending on the depth of our sincerity and how grounded we are in appropriate behavior. We cannot be sincere with inappropriate behavior, that is merely hypocrisy. In sincerity hypocrisy disappears, we ourselves determine how close we come to the truth, we ourselves know best the depth of our sincerity. We recognize our own resentment, our jealousy, we know when we are out of sorts, paranoid, angry, spiteful, hasty, out of control. If we do not know how to regain control, this is something we must learn.

When a train is going a hundred miles an hour traveling east and it wants to go west, the first thing it has to do is stop. Without stopping it cannot go in the other direction, there is too much momentum. An object in motion tends to stay in motion. There is another word to describe this, addiction, we are addicted to the way we are going. When we start by going in one direction we keep going that way, and then we think we cannot stop. That rule of physics does not have to apply to us, but it often does. We need to learn how to apply the brakes. If a train stops when it is going very fast sparks fly everywhere, there is terrible noise, a difficult process, individual cars might shake, yet it does stop as long as the brakes work. God has not given us any burdens we cannot handle. All this momentum accumulated with inappropriate ways, with our addiction to inappropriate ways, all this must come to a halt.

We must go to a place where these things are unimportant, where they have no merit, they do not make us happy or satisfy us, they do not give us a fleeting sense of peace. Recognize the place of real peace, see it, witness it, look at it. Once we see it we have to believe in it, build the certitude that it exists, that it is available. Then if we leave this place we need to know the way back, memorize the directions, have the map we have to draw for ourselves, a little different for each of us. We have different parents, a different upbringing, all the ways we have been shaped and formed, patterns of addiction requiring diversity in treatment.

There are ways to deal with the things attaching us to the surface. Once we recognize what attaches us we have to ask for forgiveness, then we can begin to do the work. Atonement, making up for our mistakes, this is repentance. What is the act of repentance? Merging, becoming one, letting go of the attachments pulling us away. Atonement or repentance means ending the separation, realizing the most important thing is our attachment to God, not to the world, realizing attachment to the world is merely illusory existence. Our attachment to God is the truth and clarity of existence, without this there is only illusion.

If we think back over our lives, think about the succession of traumas, attachments and difficulties we have encountered, one after the other, we might see our life as nothing more than a repetition of certain situations, new ones replacing the old as they withered away. When one thing is gone another pops up to take its place. The mind holds a limitless number of attachments to be obsessed with. We must release ourselves from these mental obsessions, release ourselves from these worldly attachments making us believe that reality exists in an illusory ocean we call the mind. We must give up the kind of thinking which makes us believe we get something from making progress in the world. We need a new set of values, new priorities centered here within ourselves, priorities which are deep, sincere, with no worry about what goes on out there. At the same time we are still able to do what we are supposed to do out there, we are still appropriate out there, we do our duty out there too.

There is a funny story about a three-legged goat. A man goes to visit a friend on a farm in Iowa he has not seen for twenty years. As they reminisce sitting around the kitchen table a goat with three legs runs through the kitchen. The friend asks the farmer, "Why do you have a goat living in the house with you, and why does it have only three legs?"

The farmer answers, "Well, about a year ago when my wife and I were asleep I felt something licking my toe. I woke up to see a goat, this goat was excited, disturbed. I knew something was wrong but I couldn't say what, I couldn't even figure out how he got out of his enclosure. He was making all this noise, acting as if he wanted me to follow him. I did follow him and found the silo on fire, our house was within minutes of catching fire too. We would have all died.

"Two weeks later the same thing happened again, I was asleep when I felt something licking my toe. I woke up, saw the goat, and since I knew this is a smart goat I phoned the police to tell them we had an emergency, even though I didn't know what it was. The goat led me to the outer cellar door, and I told the police, 'Something is going on in the basement, I don't know what it is, but I'm sure something is going on.' The police found two men hiding there, they had just murdered another family a few miles away, we were next. That's when I decided this goat should live in our house."

The friend said, "That explains why he is in the house, but why does he have only three legs?"

The farmer explained, "Well, a goat like that you don't eat all at once!"

The world will eat us, if we are good to the world it might eat us slowly, but it will eat us. Until we realize this, understand it deeply, we do not want to go to the other place. Once we understand we are going to be eaten, we know we must go to the other place, we must find that place beyond illusion to save our legs, our arms, our soul.

We need to develop the sincerity and determination to do this, to yearn for reality, just as we yearn for cold water in a hot, dry desert. We should understand this thirst for our Lord, understand how He alone can quench our thirst. God is merciful, may He grant us the mercy that our thirst for Him is quenched.

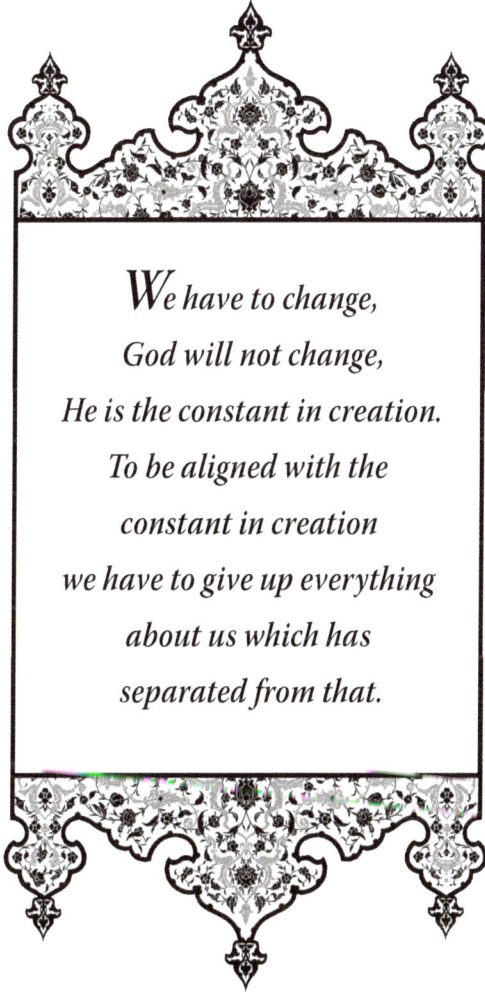

We have to change,
God will not change,
He is the constant in creation.
To be aligned with the
constant in creation
we have to give up everything
about us which has
separated from that.

God's Story, Our Story

When we read a newspaper or watch the news on television, we notice many stories have national significance. Sometimes there are individual stories, but we are usually given accounts of problems at the national level, strife or difficulties among nations, wars between countries, civil wars, migrations of peoples. The difficulties are attached to the country where the problems exist, Sudan, Iraq, Cambodia, Rwanda. This is a depersonalizing of events which makes it easier to bear what goes on—if we were told the stories of each person affected we could not watch, could not bear to contemplate it.

Yet national stories are made up of millions and millions of individual stories, we ourselves are part of such stories. We each have a story, a situation, a history which might bring tears to someone's eyes, but there is a difference between the individual story and God's story which offers an interesting way to understand our existence, to understand the world in a broader context. When we read reports of national crises we see they not only omit each individual story, they also leave out His story, they do not talk about God, they do not talk about the greater context, they never say when life ends there is another chapter to follow. They speak about nations as if they were corporations. Corporations are created to keep business going beyond the life and death of those who own or run it. In the same way, nations are independent of the life and death of individuals, nations cannot die because they are not real.

There is a joke about a group of generals standing around a map, it's an old map they say, ignore the borders. This is what the world is like, cut into slices like a pie, and when we look at an old map we find different shaped slices of the pie. We imagine the way things are and make up stories to go with what we imagine. We all have stories about the world, the one we can tell best, of course, is our own story, our own history, something we often do when we first meet someone.

Our history does have significance, an account of how we got to this moment, things we experienced bringing us to this moment. But we need to contemplate where we are at this moment, which is all we truly have, always remembering the mind is incapable of understanding this moment, of differentiating past or future from it. As long as we remain within the confines of our mind, even thinking deeply, intently, about whatever is going on, we have bypassed the moment by living in the story we need to leave behind. This is hard to do, something we can do only to a certain extent because we also live in the unreality allowing us to carry on from day to day. If we do not remember what happened yesterday our context for tomorrow is broken. This is the context of the illusion we have named history, what we have written down, what goes into our books; the whole world is identified with this illusory context. This is the way the mind works, the way the mind handles things, a familiar context.

Once we recognize there are other kinds of books, mystical books and mystical people whose function lies outside of time and place, then we know there is a story beyond the one told by the world, a different story we can understand if we lose the attachment to our individual story, our history. The less our history means to us the more we have cleared away, the more we have separated ourselves from it, now more able to grasp a true story, His story. The more we understand that His story and ours are truly connected, that they are one story, the more we understand the world's story is not the real one. Mystics tell us to be joyful in our Lord, find our happiness with God, exist in a state of praise to Him. If we are too involved in the world's story it is hard to hold onto joy and praise. Illusion denies God's omnipresence, His sanctity, bringing doubt with its questions. If God is merciful why is there war, if God is merciful why do babies die, if God is merciful why have I gone through such terror in my life?

Each of us has known difficulties. To understand God, understand that creation is a temporary manifestation. When we watch a movie we see images flickering on the screen, as soon as the lights come up the images disappear. The images we see flickering in our life all disappear too, yet our inner screen does not let them go, it retains the images we walk around with, we identify ourselves with all those images on a screen inside our head. When we go to the movies the show is over when the lights come on. The images we watch are not our life, we should not be looking for another set of images when the lights come on, we should not spend our life looking for images to attach ourselves to, making that our life, using that to create our emotion, our joy, our sorrow. When the light comes on we have a chance to go beyond images, to be with the light. We need to enter that space where images disappear and light exists, then what happens when we close our eyes to the world, when we know it is not real, not what we hold onto, then what moves us is God. We are one with Him, we disappear and He alone exists.

We have to function because we are flesh and blood, but we have been given rules about functioning appropriately. We have been told what to do, how to do it, how to act, how to be kind, how to behave. Just because we understand how to behave does not mean everyone else will too. In situations when others behave incorrectly we have been told what to do, let them go their way while we go ours. We should not be too involved with those who do not behave appropriately with us, we should learn to be independent of the way other people act, or the way we think they should. We are responsible for ourselves. When we are integrated, one within ourselves, it is easier to be joyful in our Lord.

This is a familiar story we have been told about two caliphs, 'Umar ibnul-Khaṭṭāb and Abū Bakr as-Ṣiddīq. When the prophet

Muhammad asked that charity be given, 'Umar gave half of everything he had. When Muhammad asked what he had donated, 'Umar said, "I gave half of everything I had."

Then he asked, "What about the rest?"

'Umar replied, "The rest is to take care of my family and children."

Next Muhammad asked Abū Bakr what he could give. He answered, "I will give everything I have."

The prophet Muhammad inquired, "What about your family and children?"

Abū Bakr answered, "My prophet and my Lord will care for my family and children."

Abū Bakr had nothing left, and since he had given everything away he was absent from the group around Muhammad during the next days. Worried about him, Muhammad sent 'Umar to find him. 'Umar said to Abū Bakr, "Muhammad hasn't seen you for a few days, where have you been?"

Abū Bakr answered, "When Muhammad called for charity I gave everything I had, then when I went home I gave away the last few things I had there. We have only two small pieces of cloth left in the house to do our prayers, my wife and I share them. I can't go out in public without appropriate dress."

'Umar told Abū Bakr, "Muhammad has sent for you, you should come."

Abū Bakr went to his backyard, took palm fronds from the date trees, made a skirt of palm fronds and walked to Muhammad's house. While he was on his way there the angel Gabriel, strangely dressed, was also on his way to see the prophet Muhammad.

Gabriel was wearing a skirt of palm fronds. Muhammad asked Gabriel, "Why are you dressed in a skirt of palm fronds?"

He replied, "I am not the only one dressed in palm fronds, all the angels in heaven are dressed this way to honor Abū Bakr. I have a message for him, tell Abū Bakr that if he is pleased with his Lord, his Lord is pleased with him."

When Abū Bakr arrived in his skirt of palm fronds the prophet gave him the message. Abū Bakr's response was, "I am truly pleased with my Lord," then he spun round and around. This is said to be the first sama, the first instance of whirling to invoke the divine presence.

The context of this story is not to be understood in a worldly way, there is a context which includes happenings in another world, the places and characters exist both in this world and another world. We also exist in this world and another world, and since we do, we should live knowing we are not of this world alone. As we become better at that, as we integrate the spiritual side of our existence, the God-conscious side of our existence, our individual story begins to disappear. Now we begin to heal, to become something other than what we were. This is a path of transformation, it is about change, about changing our story to His story. We are not, God alone exists, our story does not exist, His story exists. We do not exist, only God exists. The repetition of these words is a constant reexamination of our connection to God, a constant refocusing of that connection, a reexamination without being lost in the story of the world.

All it takes for us to be pulled away from God is some concern about what is happening in the world, some strong attachment to an idea, a person or event. When this attachment is stronger than our connection to Him we think we control what goes on here, we think by controlling what happens on the outside we can change what happens on the inside. The inside is changed from the inside not the outside, the work is inner, it is not of the mind, it is the work of the heart. There is a difference between the work of the mind and the work of the heart. How do we distinguish answers of the mind from answers of the heart, how do we know whether an answer is worldly or if it comes from the wisdom of the heart? The mind presents answers which twist and turn, offering doubts, but when the heart speaks the response is direct, it has clarity, as if we had always known. We have these moments of clarity as we become less interested in the story of the world, as we let it go.

The drama of the world is addictive, some have continuing dramas of personal violence—someone does something to someone who reacts, whose families and associates react. There are cultures whose foundations are tribal relationships and family and the differences among them, the need to maintain status. Such considerations are all about who we think we are, where we are, how to stay where we are. If these thoughts are paramount in our perspective we find it difficult to surrender to God. If we concentrate on staying as and where we are, on maintaining the status quo, we cannot enter His existence. We have to change, God will not change, He is the constant in creation. To be aligned with the constant in creation we have to give up everything about us which has separated from that.

Do we understand what we have to give up, are we capable of doing this? Do we like the way we are so much we say this is the way we are, the way we will always be, and that's that? We need personal honesty, a close examination, the ability to look at ourselves and manage what we see. We have been misled during our life, we thought we knew the truth and misled others, this we also find painful to recognize. If we think avoiding pain is important we will not look at this, we will turn and run. As soon as something difficult presents itself this is the end of transformation, the end of change, and we say it is time to stop, enough of this, turn on the television, have a drink, avoid the next step. We are happy to stay right here, happy to stop at this point. Those who are happy to stop can be self-righteous, even belligerent, religious wars can be born this way. Some say Jesus was the last prophet, they say Jesus was the son of God. Others say Muhammad was the last prophet, there are no sanctified beings in the world who can guide us any further. Read the written word, accept our interpretation of the world. Unless you agree with our interpretation you are disagreeing with Muhammad, you are disagreeing with Jesus, you are disagreeing with Moses, then the fundamentalism and fanaticism erupt which spark so many problems in the world.

Yet we can be just as fundamental and fanatic about our own life, about maintaining status, what we consider the integrity of our existence. We need to let it go, let it all disappear, accept a new kind of thinking. Accept the paradox of having two apparently opposite perspectives at the same time without a problem. The Qur'an offers a number of paradoxes. The prophet Muhammad recited the words in this book which we are to accept, but the same book tells us that people with another book who are truthful, who have the integrity to follow their own book will also find their way to God. There are other books, the way is available, although very few interpret the texts this way.

There is another example of paradox in the second chapter of the Qur'an, a change in the direction to face during prayer is announced. Worshipers are directed to face Mecca instead of Jerusalem, turning in the opposite direction. The Qur'anic explanation of this tells us it is not about facing east or west when we pray, it is about helping orphans, it is about giving charity, supporting our family. Whether they faced east or west to pray became so important at the time of Muhammad that many of his followers left, even as they were told it was not about facing east or west, it was about who and what we are, what we become. Everything in the world will disappear, the soul remains.

A corroded soul attached to the world cannot leave this earth to ascend, only a pure soul will ascend. Everything we take from the world corrodes us, everything we hold onto from the world corrupts us. If we want to be pure, to be free, to ascend, we have to give up everything which corrodes or corrupts us. May we be clear about what these things are, may we be rid of them and drawn to the light.

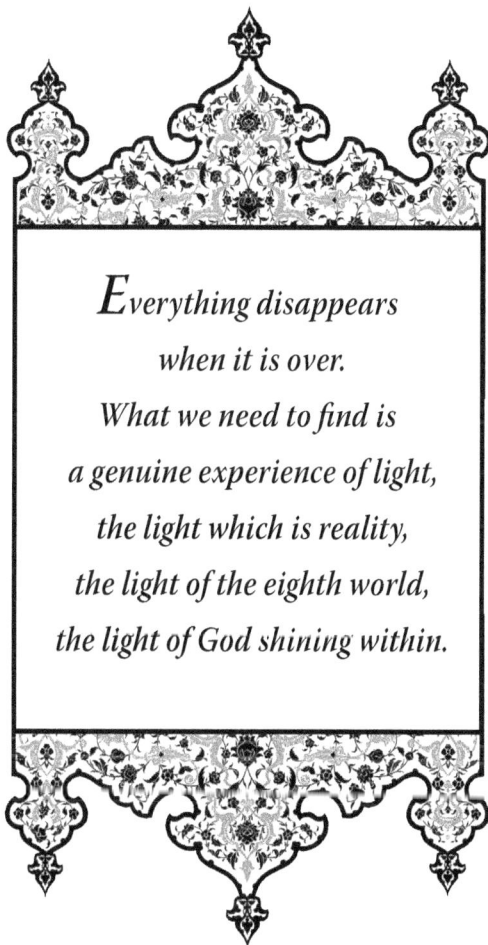

*Everything disappears
when it is over.
What we need to find is
a genuine experience of light,
the light which is reality,
the light of the eighth world,
the light of God shining within.*

CHAPTER FORTY

The Eighth World

When we study chemistry in high school one of the first things they teach us is the periodic table of elements, the different elements composing matter. They tell us everything we know is a combination of these elements. An older tradition has compressed all these elements into five, earth, air, fire, water and ether. This tradition tells us that everything we see with our physical eyes is made of these elements, everything animal, vegetable or mineral, even people. The five elements, in effect, constitute five worlds, the world of earth, the world of air, of fire, water, and the world of ether. There are two additional worlds within animals and ourselves, they are the worlds of mind and desire, but there is an eighth world which separates us from the animals, the world of light. This is not an outer world, this world of inner light exists within, beyond what the physical eye can see, this is what makes a human being the vice-regent of God. We must come to know this eighth world, the light world, we must transcend the worlds of earth, air, fire, water, ether, mind and desire.

We have to look into this world of light, inquire into it and come to know it, or we will live the life of someone who lives on the surface alone. Our life will consist of what we see, what we hear and touch, what our sensory perceptions identify, nothing deeper than that. This is equivalent to looking at the surface of the ocean and saying that is all the ocean is about, without going deeper. Anyone who has ever been scuba diving or has been in a submarine, anyone who has gone beneath the ocean's surface recognizes there is more going on underneath than above. Because so much goes on above we are inclined to believe that is all there is, we have enough to keep us occupied, very occupied. In this surface world which we see with our physical eyes there are millions of glittering illusions, millions of fascinating things to entrance us, to keep us busy. Look at the books it takes people years to write, look just for example at detailed studies of butterflies. Some can spend their lives studying butterflies or other insects, the minutiae of the physical world where there certainly is enough to study, but what have we left out if we look exclusively at these outer things? We never come to know who we are, we never come to know what goes on within if we are so busy reacting to the outer, out there in the worlds of mind and desire, the worlds of earth, fire, air, water and ether.

We have to make a break with the outer, we have to make this break deliberately and consciously. What creates a yearning to make that break? Sometimes it is the thought, is that all there is? Sometimes as we chase the world we are like a barking dog chasing the bus, if we catch it, now what? When we have that experience there is an opportunity to transcend mind and desire, but this only comes once in awhile, it can be years until it happens again. The fascinations of the world hold us in place for long periods of time.

Think about going to the movies, we are entranced, then the lights come back on, and we leave. Does the movie continue in a different way, instead of looking at the image on a screen do we think what we see now is reality, do we think the movie was an illusion and what we see now is reality? What we see is not on a screen, we can walk up to it, we can touch it, does that make it real? Just as the movie disappears when it comes to the end, everything we see will also disappear, everything we know will disappear. Everything disappears when it is over. What we need to find is a genuine experience of light, the light which is reality, the light of the eighth world, the light of God shining within.

How do we connect with that? First we have to bypass all the hooks projected by these other worlds, each hook barbed like a fishhook. When we pull it out it hurts more on the way out than it did on the way in. Every hook we remove has the pain of regret that we allowed it to confuse us so long, regret that we believed in it for such a long time, regret that we were misled, that we misled others. We are in pain as we recognize we became deceivers, liars, just as we were lied to. We have to go through the pain of regret for every mistake or misleading thing we have done, that is the barb which has to come out. If we cannot accept the pain, if we cannot face the reality of mistakes we have made, especially those committed in the name of truth before knowing what truth is, if we cannot face the illusions we helped to spread, we will not be able to pull out the hook. If we do not pull it out that hook will drag us away from moments when we do see the truth, it will drag us back to where we were.

We have spent so much of our life in illusion, but now that we have seen a mirror of reality we have to disengage. This path is the realization that we have lived in illusion, that we have lived in the worlds of mind and desire which do not actually exist. There is an ocean in the world of the mind where a self appears to exist, but there is no self, where a man appears to exist, but there is no man, where a woman appears to exist, but there is no woman, where glitters appear to exist, but there are no glitters. The only thing which exists is the ocean, and that ocean is illusion. When we recognize we have spent our life living in an ocean where nothing exists except the darkness of maya, this can lead to depression, to sadness, to anxiety, or it can help us flush away everything that came before. We flush it away as we flush the toilet, we put an end to it. We know how inadequate our life has been, now we have to learn another way.

If we are fortunate we meet a person who can show us the way forward, if we are more fortunate it will be someone who loves us, helps us, promises to pick us up if we fall, who guides us and points us in the right direction. This is a sheikh, a teacher who is willing to share his life to make our existence appropriate. Such a teacher raises us as if we were his own children, he brings us to the state of a true human being. In this process we have to believe, have the confidence there is a way out of illusion. The love of such a sheikh is the medium allowing progress, allowing our maturity to grow.

Maturity grows in love, not in qualities like haste, jealousy or anger. Anger causes the reaction which takes us back to earth, air, fire, water, ether, mind and desire. As long as we function in qualities which are reactions, which make us think we have to protect ourselves, we fall right back into illusion. Illusion makes us believe we are victims, we are trampled on, it makes us believe that things which have been done to us must be rectified, put right, and then we are right back there trying to make sense of illusion, trying to straighten out illusion. Illusion cannot be straightened out, yet it can be replaced with love. In the medium of love we have the opportunity to recover, the opportunity for our heart to melt, the opportunity for mind and desire to be stilled.

As things fall away from us, as the heart melts, an opening to the light of reality is revealed. We need to be in a safe place for this. Until we have the certitude that we are in a safe place we need someone to remind us, to help us believe we are already there, we have always been in that safe place. It is only mind and desire which frighten us, which makes us believe we are not safe. During World War II President Roosevelt said the only thing we have to fear is fear itself. Perfection always exists, the problem is our inability to see it, to understand it. We need someone to point it out, to show us how perfect, how right everything is, nothing to be afraid of.

We need to develop our certitude, our faith, we need to believe what the holy beings have told us, not the politicians. We should believe those who want nothing from us, not those who want something. What do they want? They want power, money, they want our devotion, our love, they want us to pay homage to them because they need something. We should search for those who need nothing but that light they are willing to share, who need nothing because they have everything, and they are willing to give it all away.

The path to this secret understanding is what lies in the eighth world, not what exists in the other seven. We should study the eighth world, study compassion, study mercy, patience, study contentment and love, study the truth within, not what we find on the outside. Rūmī told us not to fall in love with names, he told us to fall in love with truth. We have all fallen in love with names, we fall in love with names like Christianity, names like Judaism and Islam, but we have not fallen in love with God. We need to fall in love with God and His qualities. This is the eighth world, a path to the heavens. To reach these heavens we have to conquer the worlds of earth, fire, water, air, ether, mind and desire. Once we recognize that we have spent a lifetime studying these worlds we can give them up, we can stop studying these worlds and start studying God. May God help us in this intention, open our inner eyes to His light and bring us close to Him.

www.ingramcontent.com/pod-product-compliance
Lightning Source LLC
Chambersburg PA
CBHW051814090426

42736CB00011B/1478